At Issue

AIDS in
Developing Countries

Other Books in the At Issue Series:

At Issue

AIDS in Developing Countries

Noël Merino, Book Editor

GREENHAVEN PRESS

A part of Gale, Cengage Learning

GALE
CENGAGE Learning

Detroit • New York • San Francisco • New Haven, Conn • Waterville, Maine • London

Christine Nasso, *Publisher*
Elizabeth Des Chenes, *Managing Editor*

For more information, contact:
Greenhaven Press
27500 Drake Rd.
Farmington Hills, MI 48331-3535
Or you can visit our Internet site at gale.cengage.com

For product information and technology assistance, contact us at

Gale Customer Support, 1-800-877-4253
For permission to use material from this text or product, submit all requests online at www.cengage.com/permissions

Further permissions questions can be emailed to permissionrequest@cengage.com

Articles in Greenhaven Press anthologies are often edited for length to meet page requirements. In addition, original titles of these works are changed to clearly present the main thesis and to explicitly indicate the author's opinion. Every effort is made to ensure that Greenhaven Press accurately reflects the original intent of the authors. Every effort has been made to trace the owners of copyrighted material.

Cover image courtesy of Images.com/Corbis.

LIBRARY OF CONGRESS CATALOGING-IN-PUBLICATION DATA

AIDS in developing countries / Noël Merino, book editor.
    p. cm. -- (At issue)
  Includes bibliographical references and index.
  ISBN 978-0-7377-4671-6 (hardcover) -- ISBN 978-0-7377-4672-3 (pbk.)
  1. 1. AIDS (Disease)--Developing countries. I. I. Merino, Noël.
  HQ0000.B000 2009
  362.196'97920091724--dc22

                                                          2009038721

Printed in the United States of America
  2 3 4 5 6   15 14 13 12 11

ED062

Contents

Introduction

Acquired Immune Deficiency Syndrome (AIDS) is a disease of the human immune system caused by the Human Immunodeficiency Virus (HIV). The U.S. Centers for Disease Control and Prevention (CDC) reports that HIV is passed from one person to another when infected blood, semen, or vaginal secretions comes in contact with broken skin or mucous membranes. It can also be passed from mother to child during pregnancy, delivery, or through breast-feeding. Up until the late 1990s, people infected with HIV generally developed symptoms of AIDS within ten years of becoming infected. People do not die from HIV itself, but from one of the many infections associated with AIDS. Drugs currently available can prolong the development of AIDS in people with HIV—precisely how long these drugs can prevent advancement to AIDS remains to be seen.

The first official report of AIDS was in 1981 in the *Morbidity and Mortality Weekly Report*, published by the CDC. The cases of AIDS—unnamed as such until 1982—identified in this report are not believed to be the first cases of AIDS, but the official start to the AIDS epidemic is generally traced back to this date. It was not until 1984 that AIDS was identified as being caused by a human retrovirus, HIV. Although the precise cause of HIV infection in humans is unknown, most scientists now believe that HIV evolved from the simian immunodeficiency virus (SIV) found in primates in Africa, first spreading to humans in the early twentieth century.

According to a timeline report published by the Henry J. Kaiser Family Foundation in December 2007, the first case of AIDS in Africa was reported in 1982, and by 1985 at least one case of HIV or AIDS had been reported from each region of the world. In the United States, AIDS was the leading cause of death for all Americans aged 25 to 44 from 1994 to 1995. In

1996, the number of new AIDS cases diagnosed in the United States declined for the first time since the start of the epidemic. However, in 2002, AIDS became the leading cause of death worldwide among those aged 15 to 59.

Since its inception, the growth of the AIDS epidemic has been disproportionately worse in developing countries, particularly those in sub-Saharan Africa. The Joint United Nations Programme on HIV/AIDS (UNAIDS) calculated the adult HIV prevalence rate among adults aged 15 to 49 in 2007 and found wide disparity among countries: UNAIDS estimates that 6 out of every 1000 people, or 0.6 percent, aged 15 to 49 in the United States had HIV, whereas 21 out of every 1000 people in Belize, or 2.1 percent, were infected with HIV. No countries in the world, however, came close to the rates of HIV in sub-Saharan Africa, with 26.1 percent of people aged 15 to 49 in Swaziland, 23.9 percent in Botswana, 23.2 percent in Lesotho, and 18.1 percent in South Africa being estimated to have HIV in 2007.

There's no doubt that the rate of HIV infection is worse in sub-Saharan Africa at the present time, even if people disagree about the exact extent of the disease. HIV infection in sub-Saharan Africa defies patterns seen elsewhere where HIV infection is worse among prostitutes, intravenous drug users, and gay men—in sub-Saharan Africa, HIV is prevalent in the heterosexual population. One theory is that the cultural norm in certain sub-Saharan countries is to have a few sexual partners at a time so that even if over the course of a lifetime one has the same number of partners as someone who engages in serial monogamy (one partner at a time), the overlapping of partners creates the opportunity for more infection among a larger group. As described in a November 2007 *Washington Post* article by Helen Epstein, University of Washington Professor of Sociology and Statistics Martin Morris, in 1997, "showed mathematically that sexual networks involving long-term overlapping partnerships could create a kind of 'superhighway' for HIV, even if everyone in the network had few partners." There's no consensus about the reason for the large numbers of people infected with HIV in sub-Saharan Africa, but determining the answer to this question could be very important in determining the correct way to tackle the problem.

Addressing the issue of HIV and AIDS in developing countries is complicated by the fact that people disagree about whether or not the AIDS epidemic is getting worse or getting better. There also exists a difference of opinion about how other countries should help those living with HIV and AIDS, in addition to what should be done to curb the spread of HIV. Disagreements such as these are just a few of the topics covered in the viewpoints included in *At Issue: AIDS in Developing Countries*.

1

The Global AIDS Epidemic Is the Worst in Sub-Saharan Africa

Joint United Nations Programme on HIV/AIDS (UNAIDS)

The Joint United Nations Programme on HIV/AIDS is a joint venture of the United Nations (UN) family, bringing together the efforts and resources of ten UN system organizations in the AIDS response to help the world prevent new HIV infections, care for people living with HIV, and mitigate the impact of the epidemic.

The global percentage of adults living with HIV has leveled off, with 2.7 million new HIV infections and 2 million HIV-related deaths in 2007. Sub-Saharan Africa remains the region in the world most heavily affected by HIV, accounting for 67 percent of all people living with HIV. HIV in sub-Saharan Africa is primarily spread by heterosexual intercourse, but is also transmitted by sex workers, drug use, and male homosexual intercourse. Outside of sub-Saharan Africa, new infections of HIV are on the rise in other regions including parts of Asia and the Russian Federation.

HIV remains a global health problem of unprecedented dimensions. Unknown 27 years ago, HIV has already caused an estimated 25 million deaths worldwide and has generated profound demographic changes in the most heavily-affected countries.

Joint United Nations Programme on HIV/AIDS (UNAIDS), *2008 Report on the Global AIDS Epidemic*. Geneva, Switzerland: Joint United Nations Programme on HIV/AIDS (UNAIDS), 2008. Copyright © 2008 Joint United Nations Programme on HIV/AIDS (UNAIDS). All rights reserved. Reproduced by permission.

Key Data About HIV

The most recent international [disease] epidemiological data contain some good news. In some countries in Asia, Latin America and sub-Saharan Africa, the annual number of new HIV infections is falling. The estimated rate of AIDS deaths has also declined, in part as a result of success in expanding access to antiretroviral drugs in resource-limited settings. Yet these favourable trends are not uniformly evident, either within or between regions, underscoring the need for more comprehensive progress in implementing effective policies and programmes. . . .

Globally, there were an estimated 33 million people living with HIV in 2007.

On a global scale, the HIV epidemic has stabilized, although with unacceptably high levels of new HIV infections and AIDS deaths.

- Globally, there were an estimated 33 million [30 million–36 million] people living with HIV in 2007.

- The annual number of new HIV infections declined from 3.0 million [2.6 million–3.5 million] in 2001 to 2.7 million [2.2 million–3.2 million] in 2007.

- Overall, 2.0 million [1.8 million–2.3 million] people died due to AIDS in 2007, compared with an estimated 1.7 million [1.5 million–2.3 million] in 2001.

- While the percentage of people living with HIV has stabilized since 2000, the overall number of people living with HIV has steadily increased as new infections occur each year, HIV treatments extend life, and as new infections still outnumber AIDS deaths.

- Southern Africa continues to bear a disproportionate share of the global burden of HIV: 35% of HIV infections and 38% of AIDS deaths in 2007 occurred in that subregion. Altogether, sub-Saharan Africa is home to 67% of all people living with HIV.

- Women account for half of all people living with HIV worldwide, and nearly 60% of HIV infections in sub-Saharan Africa. Over the last 10 years, the proportion of women among people living with HIV has remained stable globally, but has increased in many regions.

- Young people aged 15–24 account for an estimated 45% of new HIV infections worldwide.

- An estimated 370 000 [330 000–410 000] children younger than 15 years became infected with HIV in 2007. Globally, the number of children younger than 15 years living with HIV increased from 1.6 million [1.4 million–2.1 million] in 2001 to 2.0 million [1.9 million–2.3 million] in 2007. Almost 90% live in sub-Saharan Africa.

HIV in Young People

The [United Nations'] *Declaration of Commitment* established a target of reducing HIV prevalence by 25% in young people (ages 15–24) in the most-affected countries by 2005. To assess progress towards this goal, 35 high-prevalence countries (with national prevalence that exceeded 3%) and four additional countries in Africa with notable prevalence levels were asked to compile data on recent trends in HIV and sexual behaviour among young people.

Given the practical difficulties of conducting HIV incidence studies, serial HIV prevalence over time in young women (ages 15–24) attending antenatal [pregnancy] clinics serves as a proxy measure for incidence, providing important indications of recent epidemiological trends.

HIV prevalence among young women attending antenatal clinics in urban or rural areas (or both) has declined since 2000–2001 in 14 of the 17 countries with sufficient data to analyse recent trends in the most-affected countries (sufficient prevalence data from three different years). These countries include the Bahamas, Benin, Burkina Faso, Burundi, Côte d'Ivoire, Kenya, Lesotho, Malawi, Namibia, Rwanda, Swaziland, the United Republic of Tanzania, and Zimbabwe. Declines in HIV prevalence exceeded 25% in seven countries. In two of these countries—Botswana and Kenya—declines occurred in both urban and rural areas. In five countries—Benin, Burkina Faso, Côte d'Ivoire, Malawi, and Zimbabwe—declines were significant only in urban areas.

Condom use has increased among young people.

In addition to HIV prevalence data, a number of countries have also tracked sexual behaviours among young people. Among the 35 high-prevalence countries, 19 countries conducted national surveys between 1990 and 2007 that provided sufficient comparative data to assess sexual behaviour trends. The percentage of both young women and men (ages 15–19) who became sexually active before their 15th birthday declined in seven countries, but increased in Haiti and Rwanda. The proportion of both young women and men (ages 15–24) who had more than one partner in the previous 12 months decreased in 10 countries and remained unchanged in two, but increased among young women in two countries and among young men in one.

Condom use has increased among young people. Among young men (ages 15–24) who had more than one partner in the previous 12 months, rates of condom use increased in 12 countries. Among their female counterparts, rates of condom use increased in eight countries. Although observed changes in behaviour are not statistically significant in every instance, overall trends show that reductions in risky behaviour have been occurring in several countries.

HIV in Sub-Saharan Africa

An estimated 1.9 million [1.6 million–2.1 million] people were newly infected with HIV in sub-Saharan Africa in 2007, bringing to 22 million [20.5 million–23.6 million] the number of people living with HIV. Two thirds (67%) of the global total of 33 million [30 million–36 million] people with HIV live in this region, and three quarters (75%) of all AIDS deaths in 2007 occurred there.

Sub-Saharan Africa's epidemics vary significantly from country to country in both scale and scope. Adult national HIV prevalence is below 2% in several countries of West and Central Africa, as well as in the horn of Africa, but in 2007 it exceeded 15% in seven southern African countries (Botswana, Lesotho, Namibia, South Africa, Swaziland, Zambia, and Zimbabwe), and was above 5% in seven other countries, mostly in Central and East Africa (Cameroon, the Central African Republic, Gabon, Malawi, Mozambique, Uganda, and the United Republic of Tanzania).

HIV Trends in Sub-Saharan Africa

Most epidemics in sub-Saharan Africa appear to have stabilized, although often at very high levels, particularly in southern Africa. Additionally, in a growing number of countries, adult HIV prevalence appears to be falling. For the region as a whole, women are disproportionately affected in comparison with men, with especially stark differences between the sexes in HIV prevalence among young people.

In southern Africa, reductions in HIV prevalence are especially striking in Zimbabwe, where HIV prevalence in pregnant women attending antenatal clinics fell from 26% in 2002 to 18% in 2006. In Botswana, a drop in HIV prevalence among pregnant 15–19-year-olds (from 25% in 2001 to 18% in 2006) suggests that the rate of new infections could be slowing. The epidemics in Malawi and Zambia also appear to have stabilized, amid some evidence of favourable behaviour changes and signs of declining HIV prevalence among women using antenatal services in some urban areas.

The estimated 5.7 million South Africans living with HIV in 2007 make this the largest HIV epidemic in the world.

HIV data from antenatal clinics in South Africa suggest that the country's epidemic might be stabilizing, but there is no evidence yet of major changes in HIV-related behaviour. The estimated 5.7 million [4.9 million–6.6 million] South Africans living with HIV in 2007 make this the largest HIV epidemic in the world. Meanwhile, the 26% HIV prevalence found in adults in Swaziland in 2006 is the highest prevalence ever documented in a national population-based survey anywhere in the world.

In Lesotho and parts of Mozambique, HIV prevalence among pregnant women is increasing. In some of the provinces in the central and southern zones of the country, adult HIV prevalence has reached or exceeded 20%, while infections continue to increase among young people (ages 15–24).

HIV prevalences in the comparatively smaller epidemics in East Africa have either reached a plateau or are receding. After dropping dramatically in the 1990s, adult national HIV prevalence in Uganda has stabilized at 5.4% [5.0%–6.1%]. However, there are signs of a possible resurgence in sexual risk-taking that could cause the epidemic to grow again. For example, the proportion of adult men and women who say they had sex with a person who was not a spouse and did not live with the respondent has grown since 1995 (from 12% to 16% for women and 29% to 36% for men).

Most of the comparatively smaller HIV epidemics in West Africa are stable or are declining—as is the case for Burkina Faso, Côte d'Ivoire, and Mali. In Côte d'Ivoire, HIV prevalence among pregnant women in urban areas fell from 10% in 2001 to 6.9% in 2005. The largest epidemic in West Africa—in Nigeria, the continent's most populous country—appears to have stabilized at 3.1% [2.3%–3.8%], according to HIV infection trends among women attending antenatal clinics.

Heterosexual intercourse remains the epidemic's driving force in sub-Saharan Africa.

HIV Transmission in Sub-Saharan Africa

Heterosexual intercourse remains the epidemic's driving force in sub-Saharan Africa. The high rate of sexual transmission has also given rise to the world's largest population of children living with HIV. However, recent epidemiological evidence has revealed the region's epidemic to be more diverse than previously thought.

Heterosexual Intercourse. According to Demographic and Health Surveys in five African countries (Burkina Faso, Cameroon, Ghana, Kenya, and the United Republic of Tanzania), two thirds of HIV-infected couples were serodiscordant, that is only one partner was infected. Condom use was found to be rare: in Burkina Faso, for example, almost 90% of the surveyed cohabiting couples said they did not use a condom the last time they had sex. A separate, community-based study in Uganda has shown that, among serodiscordant heterosexual couples, the uninfected partner has an estimated 8% annual chance of contracting HIV. Strikingly, in about 30%–40% of the serodiscordant couples surveyed, the infected partner was female. Indeed, it appears that more than half of the surveyed HIV-infected women who were married or cohabiting had been infected by someone other than their current partner.

Sex work. Sex work is an important factor in many of West Africa's HIV epidemics. More than one third (35%) of female sex workers surveyed in 2006 in Mali were living with HIV, and infection levels exceeding 20% have been documented among sex workers in Senegal and Burkina Faso. Sex work plays an important, but less central, role in HIV transmission in southern Africa, where exceptionally high background prevalence results in substantial HIV transmission during sexual intercourse unrelated to sex work.

Injecting Drug Use. Injecting drug use is a factor to some extent in several of the HIV epidemics in East and southern Africa, including Mauritius, where the use of contaminated injecting equipment is the main cause of HIV infection. In various studies, about half of the injecting drug users tested in the Kenyan cities of Mombassa (50%) and Nairobi (53%) were HIV-positive.

Sex Between Men. Several recent studies suggest that unprotected anal sex between men is probably a more important factor in the epidemics in sub-Saharan Africa than is commonly thought. In Zambia, one in three (33%) surveyed men who have sex with men tested HIV-positive. In the Kenyan port city of Mombasa, 43% of men who said they had sex only with other men were found to be living with HIV. HIV prevalence of 22% was found among the 463 men who have sex with men who participated in a study in Dakar, Senegal.

HIV in Asia

In Asia, an estimated 5.0 million [4.1 million–6.2 million] people were living with HIV in 2007, including the 380 000 [200 000–650 000] people who were newly infected that year. Approximately 380 000 [270 000–490 000] died from AIDS-related illnesses. National HIV infection levels are highest in South-East Asia, where there are disparate epidemic trends.

The epidemics in Cambodia, Myanmar and Thailand all show declines in HIV prevalence, with national HIV prevalence in Cambodia falling from 2% in 1998 to an estimated 0.9% in 2006. However, epidemics in Indonesia (especially in its Papua province), Pakistan, and Viet Nam are growing rapidly. In Viet Nam, the estimated number of people living with HIV more than doubled between 2000 and 2005. New HIV infections are also increasing steadily, although at a much slower pace, in populous countries such as Bangladesh and China. . . .

HIV in Eastern Europe and Central Asia

The estimated number of people living with HIV in Eastern Europe and Central Asia rose to 1.5 million [1.1 million–1.9 million] in 2007; almost 90% of those infected live in either the Russian Federation (69%) or Ukraine (29%). It is estimated that 110 000 [67 000–180 000] people in this region became infected with HIV in 2007, while some 58 000 [41 000–88 000] died of AIDS.

The HIV epidemic in the Russian Federation (already the largest in this region) continues to grow, although apparently at a slower pace than in Ukraine, where annual new HIV diagnoses have more than doubled since 2001. The annual numbers of newly reported HIV diagnoses are also rising in Azerbaijan, Georgia, Kazakhstan, Kyrgyzstan, the Republic of Moldova, Tajikistan, and Uzbekistan (which now has the largest epidemic in Central Asia). . . .

HIV in the Caribbean

An estimated 230 000 [210 000–270 000] people were living with HIV in the Caribbean in 2007 (about three quarters of them in the Dominican Republic and Haiti), while an estimated 20 000 [16 000–25 000] people were newly infected with HIV in this region, and some 14 000 [11 000–16 000] people died of AIDS.

HIV surveillance systems are still inadequate in several Caribbean countries, but available information indicates that most of the epidemics in the region appear to have stabilized, while a few have declined in urban areas. The latter trend is especially evident in the Dominican Republic and Haiti....

HIV in Latin America

New HIV infections in 2007 totalled an estimated 140 000 [88 000–190 000], bringing to 1.7 million [1.5 million–2.1 million] the number of people living with HIV in this region. An estimated 63 000 [49 000–98 000] people died of AIDS last year [2007].

The overall levels of HIV infections in Latin America have changed little in the past decade....

HIV in North America, Western and Central Europe

The United States of America accounted for an estimated 1.2 million [690 000–1.9 million] of the 2.0 million [1.4 million–2.8 million] people living with HIV in North America, and in Western and Central Europe in 2007. Overall in those regions, 81 000 [30 000–170 000] people were newly infected with HIV in 2007. Comparatively few people—31 000 in a range of 16 000–67 000—died of AIDS last year.

In North America, annual numbers of new HIV diagnoses have remained relatively stable over recent years, but access to life-prolonging antiretroviral therapy has led to an increase in the estimated number of people living with HIV (Public Health Agency of Canada, 2006; US Centers for Disease Control and Prevention, 2007). In Western Europe, new HIV diagnoses are increasing, as is the total number of people living with HIV (the latter also because of wide access to antiretroviral treatment)....

HIV in the Middle East and North Africa

The limited HIV information available for the Middle East and North Africa indicates that approximately 380 000

[280 000–510 000] people were living with HIV in 2007, including the 40 000 [20 000–66 000] people who were newly infected with the virus last year [2007].

With the exception of the Sudan, the epidemics in this region are comparatively small. . . .

HIV in Oceania (Australia, New Zealand, and Nearby Islands)

Overall, an estimated 74 000 [66 000–93 000] people were living with HIV in Oceania in 2007, about 13 000 [12 000–15 000] of whom were newly infected in the same year.

Most of the region's epidemics are small, except in Papua New Guinea, where the annual number of new HIV diagnoses more than doubled between 2002 and 2006, when 4017 new HIV cases were reported (National AIDS Council Secretariat [Papua New Guinea], 2007).

2

Global AIDS and HIV Figures Have Been Exaggerated

Michael Fumento

Michael Fumento is an author, journalist, photographer, and attorney specializing in science and health issues. He is the author of The Myth of Heterosexual AIDS.

The worldwide HIV infection and AIDS statistics have been exaggerated by the Joint United Nations Programme on HIV/AIDS (UNAIDS) and the World Health Organization (WHO). UN-AIDS dropped figures in 2007 to show that its previous estimates had been overblown. The drop is not due to prevention and treatment efforts, as some have claimed. AIDS alarmists have been making dire predictions for years about HIV and AIDS in Africa, which have not come true. Part of the problem is that the United Nations (UN) data collection in Africa has been flawed.

The UNAIDS program [Joint United Nations Programme on HIV/AIDS] has issued its annual report in which, finally, it doesn't say how many *more* current HIV infections there are this year [2007] than last. Rather it drops the figure by over six million from its 2006 estimate. Specifically, it went from 39.5 million to 33.2 million. Further, the Agency now admits the number of new HIV infections per year peaked way back around 1998.

Gross Exaggerations and False Predictions

For years, some of us have dared write that worldwide HIV and AIDS figures have been grossly exaggerated; that we were being lied to by just about everybody, including—or espe-cially—the UNAIDS program and the World Health Organi-zation [WHO].

For example, pious Peter Piot, executive director of the UNAIDS program since its founding, in 2004 bemoaned that "Projections now suggest that some countries in sub-Saharan Africa will face *economic collapse* unless they bring their epi-demics under control." (Emphasis added.) Obviously he knew whereof he spoke; he'd been using those exact words for at least five years.

Just last year, former President Bill Clinton told attendees at the International AIDS Conference: "It's difficult to imagine how the world can grow unless we tackle AIDS." Never mind that world population growth is fastest in areas hardest hit by AIDS.

In 1988, a high Ugandan official on ABC News' *Nightline* said that within two years his nation will "be a desert." *Nightline's* reporter declared that by 2000 "50 million Africans may have died of AIDS." Yet Uganda's population has since in-creased by over a third and is among the fastest-growing in the world. As to the 50 million death figure, seven years after that prediction was to come to fruition, the *worldwide* AIDS estimate is just over half that.

AIDS Alarmists

Those who have criticized such gross exaggerations, as I did in my 1990 book *The Myth of Heterosexual AIDS*, were labeled li-ars ourselves, whackos, racists, and variety of other colorful epithets. Now I'm being told I should gloat; but personally I'm too busy shaking my head and wondering how despite our best efforts the AIDS alarmists were able to sustain their fiction for so long.

Naturally, those alarmists are now a bit defensive.

"A number of critics have accused the UNAIDS and WHO of distorting figures in the past to push for increased funding to fight AIDS," says a press release from the International AIDS Society in Geneva. Do tell!

The group, which has been bringing you only the finest AIDS disinformation since 1988, says, "This seems an unnecessary and petty position. The fact is, the evolution of HIV prevention, treatment, and care over the past quarter century is one of the great successes of medical science."

Infections said to already have occurred never existed.

Ah! Save for the efforts of groups like theirs their awful predictions would have come true. That echoes the explanation U.S. AIDS alarmists give about why their beloved heterosexual AIDS epidemic never arrived, notwithstanding that they were insistent for years that it *already had* arrived.

Likewise, the new lowered estimate for worldwide HIV has nothing to do with "prevention, treatment, care." Infections said to already have occurred never existed.

Faulty Data Collection

For its data, the U.N. [United Nations] had relied heavily on "sentinel-site surveillance" at prenatal clinics. This system was described and faulted six years ago [November 22, 2001] in *Rolling Stone* magazine. "If a given number of pregnant women are HIV-positive, the formula says, then a certain percentage of all adults and children are presumed to be infected, too." Such an extrapolation from a small non-representative portion of the population to literally the whole world is nonsense.

And UNAIDS knew it because it had been told by a number of careful, knowledgeable scientists such as Berkeley epidemiologist Dr. James Chin.

Chin, when he worked for the U.N., was responsible for some of the earliest world AIDS forecasts. Later he watched how politics—not a virus—made those figures zoom into the stratosphere.

Three years ago [2004], Chin told me: "They [the U.N.] don't falsify per se" but "as an epidemiologist I look at these numbers and how they're derived. Every step of the way there is a range and you can choose the low end or the high end. Almost consistently the high end was chosen."

The epidemic of falsehoods coming from official organizations, NGOs, politicians, and the media has yet to peak.

And guess what? Chin, who is also author of *The AIDS Pandemic: The Collision of Epidemiology With Political Correctness, still* thinks the numbers are too high. He estimates worldwide HIV infections to be 25 million, still about eight million less than the revised estimate.

So at some point the authorities will be forced to lower the figures again. But they'll hold off as long as possible in order to continue to bring more attention to this problem at the expense of shortchanging attention and funding to other problems that are much more readily preventable, treatable, or both—such as tuberculosis and malaria.

The epidemic of falsehoods coming from official organizations, NGOs [non-governmental organizations], politicians, and the media has yet to peak.

3

The AIDS Epidemic Is Past Its Peak, Even in Africa

Margaret Wente

Margaret Wente is a columnist for Canada's largest national daily newspaper, The Globe & Mail.

Statistics released in 2007 that show a drop in new HIV infections and a drop in the number of people with HIV are due to incorrect previous estimates. The peak of the AIDS epidemic was in the 1990s, with the main epidemic currently centered within Africa. Despite dire warnings, HIV has not spread too far in the general population outside of Africa. In the world outside of Africa, it is mainly gay men, intravenous drug users, and female prostitutes who are at risk of contracting HIV. The pandemic in Africa is still bad, but improving—and is not the worst pandemic to ever hit.

For the past decade, United Nations [UN] scientist Peter Piot has been sounding the alarm about the growing scourge of AIDS. "The pandemic and its toll are outstripping the worst predictions," he warned last year [2006]. "[It] is now one of the make-or-break forces of this century." The Western world has responded, with AIDS funding that has swelled to $10-billion a year.

But this week [November 2007] brought some surprising news about the epidemic. It's shrinking. Annual new HIV infections have plunged by 40 per cent, to 2.5 million. And the total number of people infected with HIV has also fallen—down to 33 million from 40 million.

What happened? Are prevention programs finally working? Has someone found a cure?

An Epidemic in Decline

Not exactly. What happened was that the UN's top AIDS scientists were finally forced to admit that their numbers had been wildly overstated. "They had clearly been using inflated numbers for some years," charged Stephen Lewis, the former special UN envoy for HIV-AIDS in Africa. He even accused UNAIDS [Joint United Nations Programme on HIV/AIDS] of being "irresponsible."

Dr. James Chin of UC [University of California] Berkeley has been tracking the disease since it first emerged. He is among the many epidemiologists who say the UN agency has cooked the numbers in order to get political and economic support. "I call them glorious lies and myths, because they're for a good cause," he told me.

Both Mr. Lewis and Dr. Chin are quick to stress that AIDS is still a huge challenge and a monumental human tragedy. But the distortion of information has caused scarce public health resources to be wasted on programs aimed at people who simply aren't at risk. Meantime, the UN's relentless fear-mongering has spread abundant misconceptions about the disease. Here are a few of the more startling facts I learned from a conversation with Dr. Chin.

The AIDS epidemic is past its peak. Even UNAIDS has admitted that global HIV incidence had peaked by the late 1990s. This doesn't mean people will stop getting AIDS any time soon. But the infection rates are on the decline. The impact of prevention programs pales beside what's known as the saturation effect—meaning that people at the most risk have already been infected. Although prevention programs get the credit, one scientist has called this phenomenon "riding to glory on the down slope of the epidemic curve."

AIDS is not a big problem outside Africa. (The continent still accounts for three-quarters of the world's AIDS deaths.) Despite widespread warnings that AIDS was about to explode across India, China and Southeast Asia, it hasn't. The UN has slashed its estimate of the HIV-infected population of India by almost two-thirds, back to 2.5 million. China has only a few hundred thousand infected people, not the millions that were predicted. Indonesia and the Philippines, where male circumcision is the norm, have escaped relatively unscathed, because circumcision is a major barrier to infection. The global infection rate outside of Africa is 0.2 per cent, says Dr. Chin. He thinks the UN numbers are still too high, and that the total number of infected might be as low as 22 million.

AIDS is not a big problem outside Africa.

Infection by High-Risk Behaviour

Outside Africa, people in the general population are unlikely to become infected. In the rest of the world, HIV is almost entirely confined to men who have sex with other men, intravenous drug users and female sex workers. That's an inconvenient truth for activists and fundraisers. "When you're trying to get the public and policy makers to take note, they're not going to be too keen on pouring money into men having sex with men and junkies and sex workers," says Dr. Chin. He says a lot of effort and money have been wasted on programs directed at the general population.

The main driver of infection is not poverty, but high-risk sexual behaviour. In Africa, the richest countries have the highest infection rates, and richer people have much higher rates than poor ones. HIV hits hardest at Africa's teachers and professionals. In the West, where the biggest at-risk group is men who have sex with men, income isn't a factor either. "No matter how you look at it, poverty isn't driving it," says Dr. Chin.

The riskiest behaviour is having multiple concurrent sexual partners. People with several overlapping sexual partners—a common practice in Africa—are at much higher risk. Westerners may have more sexual partners over a lifetime, but what matters is the pattern of behaviour. The single most effective way to reduce the spread of AIDS is partner reduction, or "mutual faithfulness."

Even in sub-Saharan Africa, the news isn't all bad.

Good News in Sub-Saharan Africa

Even in sub-Saharan Africa, the news isn't all bad. The HIV infection rate has levelled off at about 3 per cent (Dr. Chin's estimate), which means that 97 per cent of the population is not infected. In Rwanda, for example, the infection rate is now thought to be 3 per cent, down from 14 per cent or even more. This is not to minimize the devastation: Africa has more than 11 million AIDS orphans, and in some countries, the death rates among the most educated and productive people are 20 or 30 per cent. In some places, the adult prevalence rate will be at least 5 to 10 per cent for decades to come. "On the ground, the situation in Africa is still appalling," says Stephen Lewis.

AIDS is a terrible pandemic, but it's not the worst. Tuberculosis wiped out up to a billion people over the 18th and 19th centuries. Malaria kills a million people every year, mostly children under 5. Nor is AIDS a general killer. Unlike an influenza epidemic, which can infect up to half the population, it only hits selected subgroups.

And yet, a lot of people don't want to hear the (relatively) good news about AIDS. Dr. Chin and others who challenge the official line tend to be denounced for being callous and cold-hearted. After all, the global competition for dollars is fierce, and the stakes are huge. But Dr. Chin points out that in the end, fudging the facts doesn't help anyone—least of all the victims of this tragic, dreadful plague.

4

Treatment for HIV and AIDS in Developing Countries Involves Challenges

AVERT

AVERT is an international HIV and AIDS charity based in the United Kingdom, working to eliminate HIV and AIDS worldwide.

People with HIV in developing countries can benefit from antiretroviral medications if challenges to treatment can be overcome. The cost of antiretroviral drug treatment has declined in recent years, but still needs to become more inexpensive to reach all those needing treatment in the developing world. Other challenges to successful drug treatment include getting people tested, getting people to adhere to treatment, having the necessary infrastructure and workforce to deliver treatment, and reaching patients regardless of location or other barrier. These challenges can be overcome to save the lives of millions of people.

Though massive strides have been made in scaling-up antiretroviral treatment, it is clear that far more progress is needed to achieve anything nearing universal access. There are many constraints on achieving such ambitious targets, with costs and financial resources being at the centre.

Universal access is broadly defined. It does not necessarily mean 100% coverage of all services but can be seen as a desire to move to a high level of access for the most effective inter-

Matthew Leake, "Universal Access to Aids Treatment: Targets and Challenges," Avert.org, June 2009. Reproduced by permission.

ventions that are 'equitable, accessible, affordable, comprehensive and sustainable over the long-term'. Over 100 countries have set their own 2010 universal access targets with most countries aiming for 80% treatment coverage.

Cost of HIV Treatment

It is estimated that to achieve universal treatment targets an investment of $7 billion will be required in 2010 for treatment and care alone. This is of the estimated $25 billion needed to achieve all targets including prevention, care for orphans and vulnerable children, and other programme support costs. Considering less than $14 billion was invested in tackling HIV and AIDS in 2008, a funding shortfall, while not inevitable, is likely unless dramatic increases in financial commitments are made. The Global Fund expects to be $4 billion short of the amount it requires by 2010, and PEPFAR [President's Emergency Fund for AIDS Relief] spending was not significantly increased in President [Barack] Obama's 2010 budget, reflecting concerns that funding would flat-line.

> *HIV prevention programmes are likely to be affected, inevitably increasing the number of people requiring treatment.*

In a global economic downturn, the prospect of greater funding for AIDS appears uncertain. In a 2009 World Bank survey of 69 countries, one third expected to see AIDS treatment programmes negatively affected over the year. Treatment programmes in sub-Saharan Africa were predicted to experience the worst of the financial crisis. Indirect impacts of the financial crisis on treatment programmes could come in the form of increased poverty levels leading to more risky behaviours such as trading sex for money. Adequate nutrition, which is vital for people on ARVs [antiretroviral drugs], could also decline leading to ineffective treatment. In South Africa, some private sector funding, especially from the mining sector, is being cut. Although business has committed funding for treatment programmes, HIV prevention programmes are likely to be affected, inevitably increasing the number of people requiring treatment.

Another financial barrier to universal treatment access is that once people begin taking ARVs, they must continue taking them for life. This could mean a commitment on the part of governments or international donors to guarantee treatment for many decades, for every person on ARVs.

Continuing to guarantee treatment for those who need it means treatment numbers will only grow unless people die or stop taking ARVs. Removing the life-line of antiretroviral therapy (ART) from individual patients is unlikely to be an option for governments. Therefore, overall health or HIV/ AIDS budgets will have to grow with this expansion of treatment, or the share of these budgets will have to shift in favour of treatment, at the expense of prevention or care services. Alternatively, other public spending would have to be redirected.

Someone with a CD4 count of 300 in the UK, for example, would be considered in need of treatment, whereas someone with a similarly advanced infection in a less developed country may not be regarded as needing treatment.

When Treatment Should Begin

Another aspect of treatment access to consider is at what point people with HIV become eligible for treatment. In more economically developed countries, the threshold for treatment is a CD4 count (a level of a type of immune cell) that has dropped below 350 cells per cubic millimetre of blood. In less developed countries, treatment does not begin until the CD4 count drops below 200.

The stage of infection at which people are eligible to begin taking ARVs provides some context to the percentage of people regarded as in 'need' of treatment. Someone with a CD4 count of 300 in the UK [United Kingdom], for example, would be considered in need of treatment, whereas someone with a similarly advanced infection in a less developed country may not be regarded as needing treatment. The levels of investment and resources that are necessary to obtain a certain level of access to treatment are therefore very much linked to a country's definition of need.

Deferring treatment until infection has progressed may seem a cheaper option for funders of treatment programmes, but some say that initiating treatment earlier may be cost-effective in the long run. They argue the costs of a deferred treatment approach are 'substantially increased' by intensive clinical care, having to make more likely switches to expensive second-line treatment, an increased infection rate, and the loss of patients' economic productivity. Despite the potential cost savings, treating patients earlier would inevitably require greater initial spending on antiretroviral drugs. Therefore it is debatable whether most governments would be prepared to make changes to their guidelines that would appear to boost costs and extend treatment waiting lists.

Allocating Resources

Establishing guidelines as to who is entitled to HIV treatment, when, and with which ARVs, is a way of allocating, often scarce, resources. Short of treating everyone who needs treatment, the question remains over how to ration the resources needed for HIV treatment programmes. There are various ways that this can be done.

Firstly, particular demographics can be targeted for treatment. These could include mothers of new infants in order to prevent the child from becoming an AIDS orphan; skilled workers such as teachers, police, judges and civil servants regarded as contributing to economic productivity or social stability; the poorest people least able to fund their own treatment privately; and high-risk populations in order to suppress the level of HIV and consequently reduce onward transmission.

For example, in 2005 Ugandan civil servants became eligible for free ARV drugs, with a government minister claiming that such workers' "expertise is not easily replicated". A PEPFAR-supported scheme targeted military personnel in Nigeria. In the US, the Ryan White HIV/AIDS Program targets those who do not have health insurance or sufficient financial resources.

Other forms of rationing include targeting people who live in particular areas such as those which perhaps have a high HIV prevalence or are politically important, prioritising treatment to those who can partially fund it, and limiting treatment to those who can demonstrate a degree of commitment to ARV adherence.

Rationing can also take place without overt restrictions on access to HIV treatment or programmes directed at particular groups. The time and costs involved in travelling a substantial distance to testing or treatment sites will implicitly favour those who live nearby or have more spare time. Furthermore, any groups who are not targeted for testing, which is necessary before treatment, are indirectly restricted from treatment programmes. Those with power and influence are also likely to be able to take advantage of any rationing system.

The potential positive and negative aspects of each system must be weighed against each other when deciding how to allocate antiretroviral treatment.

Reaching Patients

Establishing when, how and who initiates treatment is one set of issues in getting people with HIV on antiretroviral therapy. However, keeping people on treatment programmes—patient retention—should be considered as important a factor as boosting the numbers of people beginning treatment.

Patients who no longer continue with treatment are often classified as "lost to follow-up". This could be for a range of possible reasons including simply stopping or interrupting treatment, death, or finding alternative sources of ARVs. The nature of loss to follow-up is that very often a patient's eventual whereabouts or outcome is unknown, even if efforts are made to trace such patients.

In a review of studies examining patient retention in antiretroviral therapy programmes in Africa, just 60% of patients remained with their programme after two years. The remainder were lost to follow-up or had died. Another study examining data on 5,491 patients beginning antiretroviral therapy in 15 treatment programmes in Africa, South America and Asia, found 21% of patients became lost within six months, including 4% who were not seen since receiving their first prescription of ARVs.

Some studies suggest that patient retention actually suffers as a result of the drive to boost patient initiation. The research across three continents found the proportion of patients who were lost to follow-up was greater in 2003–2004 than in 2000 or earlier. This, it was suggested, was due to difficulties following-up the growing patient numbers.

Challenges for Treatment

A variety of factors influence why individuals discontinue their treatment. Cost has a major impact on patient retention and mortality levels. Similarly, associated costs such as transportation or "opportunity costs" such as having to forgo a day's pay are other more structural factors. Adverse side effects of ARVs may cause someone to stop taking them, as could successful therapy if it leads people to become complacent.

Another set of social, cultural and psychological influences should also be considered. Perceptions of disease severity, susceptibility and the benefits or disadvantages of staying on treatment are key in determining clinical attendance. Believing that God or alternative medicine can cure AIDS can also influence treatment patterns. Similarly, misconceptions about ARVs can alter patients' motivation to stick with them.

If drug resistance occurs through failure to adhere to ARVs, far more expensive second-line therapy, may be necessary.

Nutritional support is vital too as a lack of adequate food security could determine whether people remain on treatment. Some medications can only be taken on a full stomach while some ARV side effects are reduced by having adequate nutrition.

Sticking to a treatment regimen for life that involves taking daily medication, with potential side effects, presents many challenges that must be overcome if patients are to successfully remain on treatment. If drug resistance occurs through failure to adhere to ARVs, far more expensive second-line therapy, may be necessary.

Having supportive family and community environments, as well as strong networks of people living with HIV are key to promoting adherence to ARV treatment. This could come in the form of very practical assistance such as transport to a clinic or help with other activities. Patients may require emotional support to continue their treatment both from their family and HIV-positive peers. The success of other people on ARVs can encourage patients to continue with their therapy.

Before people can be treated they need to know they are infected. This requires not only HIV testing facilities but also widespread knowledge of the importance of testing and where it can be done. People may be more inclined to test if they know of the benefits of antiretroviral therapy and know they could be treated in the event of testing positive. Confronting stigma and denial are absolutely necessary as these are 'the two factors that often determine whether a person seeks an HIV test or not', according to the former South African health minister.

On average, there are 15 times the number of doctors and 8 times the number of nurses in Europe compared to Africa.

Health Worker Shortages

Many health staff are required at various stages of a treatment programme including for testing and assessment, and ARV prescription. However, countries with higher HIV prevalence tend to have lower health staff-to-patient ratios compared with more developed countries. Malawi, for example, has just one doctor per 50,000 people compared to the United States with one per 390 people. On average, there are 15 times the number of doctors and 8 times the number of nurses in Europe compared to Africa.

There are several reasons for this, one of which is AIDS itself. In Botswana, for example, 17% of the health-care workforce died due to AIDS between 1999 and 2005.

Migration of health staff from poorer to wealthier countries has also damaged the health infrastructure of countries ravaged by AIDS. It has even been suggested that the widespread recruitment of African health workers by more developed countries should be viewed as an 'international crime'.

One proposal for tackling HIV with diminished staff capacity is to train or permit lesser-qualified health workers to perform tasks which they were previously unqualified to do. This is known as 'task-shifting'. Allowing nurses to perform some of the tasks of doctors, and community workers the roles of nurses, for example, could facilitate access to ART and improve adherence and management of therapy. It is argued that quality of care would not be compromised and that it could be more cost-effective than the present division of labour. Task-shifting has existed in Zambia, for example, since 2004, but has yet to be implemented in South Africa despite the National Strategic Plan (NSP) calling for such measures.

Reliable Supply Chains Needed

Ensuring there are no interruptions in treatment requires a guaranteed supply of antiretroviral drugs from the factories where they are produced to the treatment centres in perhaps remote areas of a country. Laboratory supplies, testing kits and information also needs to pass along the supply chain.

In order to be cost-effective, accurate forecasting of the necessary quantity of drugs is needed. Over-purchasing of ARVs can put strains on money and storage space, and may lead to wasting of drugs with limited shelf-life. Under-estimating may lead to stockouts and the need to purchase costlier emergency supplies. One report found stockouts were 'commonplace' in China, India, Uganda, Russia and Zimbabwe. It was conservatively estimated that 30 people were dying daily in Free State, South Africa, after ARVs ran out towards the end of the 2009 financial year. Such events not only adversely affect those who desperately need to begin treatment but also patients who were on treatment already and who may develop drug resistance.

Quantification and procurement of drugs is trickier for HIV than other areas of public health due to the changing nature of the epidemic, evolving efforts to tackle it, particularly with regards to scaling-up treatment, and changes in the price and quality of drugs.

The transportation phase of the supply chain requires delivery tracking and needs to account for potential customs barriers. Special refrigerated containers may also be needed. In unstable regions theft of the drugs may be a concern and armed escorts and decoy trucks are known to protect expensive deliveries.

Intermediate storage of the medication—such as in large regional warehouses—needs to be safe and secure and be able to efficiently process orders and distribute ARVs to health facilities. Similarly, local facilities should be able to safely and securely store medication often at controlled temperatures.

The massive international logistical exercise involved in creating a reliable supply chain for thousands of vital deliveries has meant the consortium that operates PEPFAR's supply chain, the Supply Chain Management System, was the organisation that received the most money from the initiative in the 2007 financial year.

It goes without saying that HIV treatment programmes need a steady supply of drugs. However, the quality and type of drugs that are available will also have an impact on the effectiveness of the programme. Treatment regimens in most developing countries are based on a drug called stavudine, or d4T, which has severe side effects that have led to its discontinued use in richer countries. Such side effects may dissuade patients from taking their medication, whereas better quality, though often more expensive, ARVs may encourage people to continue treatment and could require fewer costly treatment switches.

Other medical supplies besides the antiretroviral drugs are also required. In developed countries, decisions about when to start treatment are based on the results of clinical tests called the CD4 test and the viral load test. Ideally these tests should be used everywhere, but in many parts of the world they are currently unavailable, as they require expensive equipment, electricity and trained technicians. In theory, decisions about when to start treatment may be based on symptoms alone. However, in practice, some treatment programmes provide medication only to people who have had a CD4 count.

Moving Forward

Significant progress has been made in getting millions of people on treatment. Over 3 million life years have been gained since 2002, including 2 million in sub-Saharan Africa thanks to antiretroviral therapy. Treatment expansion has led to seven-and-a-half times as many people on treatment in low and middle-income countries by the end of 2007 (around 3 million) compared with 2003 (around 400,000).

Treatment will also need to be made more accessible through decentralizing entry points to care, task-shifting, and generally having well functioning health systems.

However, it is clear that in order to realise universal access to treatment, the scale of the task will have to be made easier through effective prevention to drastically reduce new infections.

Treatment will also need to be made more accessible through decentralising entry points to care, task-shifting, and generally having well functioning health systems. Adherence and retention rates will have to be improved both for the health of the patients and so that it is worth the vast and unprecedented financial investment in getting individuals on treatment. All of this will require huge investment and commitment from governments, donors and international organisations. Though it is uncertain whether all of this will be implemented, it is certain that without such factors, universal treatment access will remain elusive.

5

Women and Children in Sub-Saharan Africa Suffer Greatly from AIDS

Peter Gyves

Peter Gyves is a Jesuit priest at St. Ignatius Loyola Parish in New York City and a member of the Society of Jesus. He provides medical assistance to poor children in Africa and Asia during the summer months.

While two-thirds of those living with HIV in the world are located in sub-Saharan Africa, the picture is even worse for women and children: Approximately three-quarters of women with HIV are in sub-Saharan Africa, and 90 percent of the world's HIV-positive children live in sub-Saharan Africa. The main issue driving the large percentage of children with HIV is the high level of mother-to-child transmission. The numbers of sub-Saharan women and children with HIV, and mortality associated with the disease, could be lowered by pursuing several goals that would help to both prevent HIV infection in women and lower rates of mother-to-child transmission.

In sub-Saharan Africa, where antiretroviral therapy has increased more than eightfold since the end of 2003, great strides are being made in treating patients with H.I.V./AIDS. Those in the know, like participants in the 16th International AIDS Conference held last April [2006] in Toronto, Canada, express great optimism about treating the disease in the developing world. The United Nations' Global Fund, the U.S. president's Emergency Plan for AIDS Relief and the Bill and Melinda Gates Foundation have directed funds to this part of the world and made rapid progress possible. Although such optimism is largely justified, much work remains to be done, especially in preventing and treating H.I.V./AIDS in children.

Progress in preventing and treating the disease in children lags far behind the advances made in treating adults.

Visits to African Hospitals

Over the past three years, I have visited Kenya, Chad, South Africa and Zambia to understand better the changes taking place in the care of people infected by H.I.V. What I have learned is that progress in preventing and treating the disease in children lags far behind the advances made in treating adults, and that among adults men fare significantly better than women.

During a recent visit to the university teaching hospital in Lusaka, the capital of Zambia, I met with staff physicians responsible for the care of children admitted with a variety of illnesses, including H.I.V./AIDS. I accompanied the chief pediatrician as she examined a child—H.I.V. positive, with severe anemia and malnutrition—and noticed another physician across the ward applying oxygen to an infant. By the time we approached this baby and her mother, the examining physician had just removed the oxygen from the child's face. The mother began to cry as a nurse wrapped the infant in a sheet and carried her away; her tiny daughter had died before much could be done to help her. The mother had brought her, in severe respiratory distress, to the hospital from an outlying clinic, because it had been unable to care for her baby. The examining physician told us that the infant was about 4 months old and appeared wasted. He thought it possible, even likely, that both the infant and her mother were H.I.V. positive and that the baby had died from an untreated AIDS-related pneumonia. Neither the mother's nor the infant's H.I.V. status was known.

This sad but familiar scenario, one I had seen several times before in visits to sub-Saharan Africa, was an unpleasant reminder that despite increased access to antiretroviral therapy in this part of the world, childhood death is frequently H.I.V.-related.

AIDS Devastation in Sub-Saharan Africa

The magnitude of the problem is striking. Since AIDS was first recognized in 1981, H.I.V. has infected 65 million people and killed 25 million of them. Today [2006] 38.6 million people live with H.I.V. Of these, 24.5 million—64 percent of the world's total—are in sub-Saharan Africa, an area that contains only 10 percent of the world's population.

The number of children with H.I.V. worldwide is directly linked to the number of pregnant women with the disease, and mother-to-child transmission is the most common way that children become infected.

Women and children suffer disproportionately. For example, 75 percent of all women with H.I.V. live in sub-Saharan Africa; they account for almost 60 percent of the adults living with the disease there. Despite this, only 6 percent of pregnant women in sub-Saharan Africa are offered treatment to prevent mother-to-child transmission of the virus. It is not surprising then that some 2 million children in the region live with H.I.V., which is almost 90 percent of the world's H.I.V.-infected children. Still, only 7 percent of the people receiving antiretroviral therapy in sub-Saharan Africa are children.

Among the enormous consequences of H.I.V. infection in the region are an estimated 12 million orphans.

Mother-to-Child Transmission

The number of children with H.I.V. worldwide is directly linked to the number of pregnant women with the disease, and mother-to-child transmission is the most common way that children become infected. In the United States, the near universal access of pregnant women to a combination of antiretroviral therapy and intensive surveillance of those treated has reduced the transmission rate to approximately 1 percent (down from 25 percent before antiretroviral therapy was provided).

What a contrast to the situation in sub-Saharan Africa, where access to such preventive programs is limited. Access varies from country to country and within countries and reflects the financial resources of a country, access to treatment centers of any kind, problems in identifying H.I.V.-positive pregnant women and varying levels of training among the health personnel who deliver and monitor the programs. Moreover, mother-to-child prevention programs in sub-Saharan Africa usually offer pregnant women a single dose of antiretroviral therapy at the onset of labor and one dose to the newborn within the first 72 hours of life. This strategy has decreased the mother-to-child transmission of H.I.V. from approximately 25 percent to 11 percent. The simplified, shorter course of antiretroviral therapy is related to cost and the inherent difficulties in monitoring those receiving treatment.

Breast-feeding by H.I.V.-positive women is problematic. It increases the risk of transmitting the virus to babies by 5 to 15 percent over their first two years of life. Consequently, in sub-Saharan Africa the overall risk that mothers who have not received preventive treatment will transmit the virus to their newborns reaches 30 to 40 percent. Even the women benefitting from prevention therapy still incur a risk of some 15 to

25 percent. Despite the additional risk, the practice of breast feeding continues to be encouraged, because it protects against bacterial intestinal infections and ultimately carries less risk of death to H.I.V.-positive infants than do the alternatives: using formulas and solid foods during the early months of life.

A worldwide view of H.I.V. infection in children sees two very different worlds. While few infants with H.I.V. are currently being born in the United States, the number of infected infants born in sub-Saharan Africa remains alarmingly high. The nearly universal availability of programs to prevent mother-to-child transmission in the United States is further enhanced by physicians' ability to identify H.I.V.-positive infants quickly and to offer high-tech treatment. Caregivers can quantify the amount of H.I.V. in the body, monitor drug levels to ensure a therapeutic effect, determine whether the virus is resistant to individual antiretroviral drugs and provide access to newer classes of antiretrovirals and antibiotics.

In sub-Saharan Africa, by contrast, identifying H.I.V. in infants is mostly limited to antibody testing, which often produces false positive results during the first 18 months of life because of interference from maternal antibodies. While treatment in this setting usually consists of a variation of the combination antiretroviral drugs used in the United States, surveillance remains a major obstacle. Issues range from the need to refrigerate some antiretroviral drugs to the prohibitive costs of high-tech laboratory testing and medicines.

U.S. standards for the prevention and treatment of children with H.I.V. are unrealistic for sub-Saharan Africa at the present time.

Attainable Goals for Women and Children

U.S. standards for the prevention and treatment of children with H.I.V. are unrealistic for sub-Saharan Africa at the present time. Still, several attainable goals would significantly lower the prevalence of H.I.V. in children there and increase the survival time of children already infected.

Here are some of them:

1. Increase dramatically the percentage of pregnant women enrolled in programs to prevent mother-to-child transmission (the current level is only 6 percent). These programs must also move toward the combination drug therapy and surveillance system offered in the United States.

2. Make the prevention and treatment of all women with H.I.V. a high priority.

3. Improve the general health care of H.I.V.-infected children, especially those under the age of 2. Improvement would include timely immunization against common childhood diseases and reducing the prevalence of malnutrition, tuberculosis and the most common causes of child deaths in the developing world—malaria and intestinal and respiratory diseases.

4. Provide care and monitoring for children who need combination antiretroviral therapy. That would entail a commitment to increase significantly the percentage of children receiving the therapy (from the current level of 7 percent) and a shift toward more high-tech treatment.

5. Encourage governments of the developed and developing worlds to respond to the plight of children with H.I.V. in sub-Saharan Africa, allocating more H.I.V. funding for children and pregnant women.

Without progress in these areas, large numbers of children in sub-Saharan Africa will continue to be born with H.I.V. and to die long before their time. The current contrast demonstrates that the story of children with H.I.V./AIDS is a tale of two very different worlds. The achievement of the developed world in preventing and treating children with H.I.V. is arguably the greatest success story to date in the struggle to control AIDS, yet it stands as a tragedy alongside the number of children who are dying of the same disease in the developing world.

6

There Are Much Bigger Health Concerns in Developing Countries than AIDS

Daniel Halperin

Daniel Halperin is a lecturer on international health in the Department of Global Health and Population at the Harvard School of Public Health.

American foreign assistance for HIV/AIDS is out of proportion to the threat HIV/AIDS poses in developing countries. Millions of Africans die of preventable conditions such as diarrhea from unclean water, yet a very small percentage of American foreign health assistance goes to fund clean water initiatives. Other examples in Africa show how a high level of funding for HIV/ AIDS sometimes even worsens the problem of mortality from preventable conditions. The United States needs to rethink its global health priorities in giving assistance to developing countries, and stop overfocusing on HIV and AIDS.

Although the United Nations recently lowered its global H.I.V. estimates, as many as 33 million people worldwide are still living with the AIDS virus. This pandemic requires continued attention; preventing further deaths and orphans remains imperative. But the well-meaning promises of some [2008] presidential candidates to outdo even President [George

W.] Bush's proposal to nearly double American foreign assistance to fight AIDS strike me, an H.I.V.-AIDS specialist for 15 years, as missing the mark.

Spending on HIV Abroad

Some have criticized Mr. Bush for requesting "only" $30 billion for the next five years for AIDS and related problems, with the leading Democratic candidates having pledged to commit at least $50 billion if they are elected. Yet even the current $15 billion in spending represents an unprecedented amount of money aimed mainly at a single disease.

Many other public health needs in developing countries are being ignored.

Meanwhile, many other public health needs in developing countries are being ignored. The fact is, spending $50 billion or more on foreign health assistance does make sense, but only if it is not limited to H.I.V.-AIDS programs.

Last year [2007], for instance, as the United States spent almost $3 billion on AIDS programs in Africa, it invested only about $30 million in traditional safe-water projects. This nearly 100-to-1 imbalance is disastrously inequitable—especially considering that in Africa H.I.V. tends to be most prevalent in the relatively wealthiest and most developed countries. Most African nations have stable adult H.I.V. rates of 3 percent or less.

Many millions of African children and adults die of malnutrition, pneumonia, motor vehicle accidents and other largely preventable, if not headline-grabbing, conditions. One-fifth of all global deaths from diarrhea occur in just three African countries—Congo, Ethiopia and Nigeria—that have relatively low H.I.V. prevalence. Yet this condition, which is not particularly difficult to cure or prevent, gets scant attention from the donors that invest nearly $1 billion annually on AIDS programs in those countries.

Other Health Needs in Africa

I was struck by this discrepancy between Western donors' priorities and the real needs of Africans last month [December 2007], during my most recent trip to Africa. In Senegal, H.I.V. rates remain under 1 percent in adults, partly due to that country's early adoption of enlightened policies toward prostitution and other risky practices, in addition to universal male circumcision, which limits the heterosexual spread of H.I.V. Rates of tuberculosis, now another favored disease of international donors, are also relatively low in Senegal, and I learned that even malaria, the donors' third major concern, is not quite as rampant as was assumed, with new testing finding that many fevers aren't actually caused by the disease.

Meanwhile, the stench of sewage permeates the crowded outskirts of Dakar, Senegal's capital. There, as in many other parts of West Africa and the developing world, inadequate access to safe water results in devastating diarrheal diseases. Shortages of food and basic health services like vaccinations, prenatal care and family planning contribute to large family size and high child and maternal mortality. Major donors like the President's Emergency Plan for AIDS Relief, known as Pepfar, and the Global Fund to Fight AIDS, Tuberculosis and Malaria have not directly addressed such basic health issues. The Global Fund's director, Michel Kazatchkine, has acknowledged, "We are not a global fund that funds local health."

Botswana, which has the world's most lucrative diamond industry and is the second-wealthiest country per capita in sub-Saharan Africa, is nowhere near as burdened as Senegal with basic public health problems. But as one of a dozen Pepfar "focus" countries in Africa, this year it will receive about $300 million to fight AIDS—in addition to the hundreds of millions already granted by drug companies, private foundations and other donors. While in that sparsely populated country last month, I learned that much of its AIDS money remains unspent, as even its state-of-the-art H.I.V. clinics cannot absorb such a large influx of cash.

As the United States Agency for International Development's H.I.V. prevention adviser in southern Africa in 2005 and 2006, I visited villages in poor countries like Lesotho, where clinics could not afford to stock basic medicines but often maintained an inventory of expensive AIDS drugs and sophisticated monitoring equipment for their H.I.V. patients. H.I.V.-infected children are offered exemplary treatment, while children suffering from much simpler-to-treat diseases are left untreated, sometimes to die.

If one were to ask the people of virtually any African village what their greatest concerns are, the answer would undoubtedly be the . . . ravages of hunger, dirty water and environmental devastation.

Questionable Global Health Priorities

In Africa, there's another crisis exacerbated by the rigid focus on AIDS: the best health practitioners have abandoned lower-paying positions in family planning, immunization and other basic health areas in order to work for donor-financed H.I.V. programs.

The AIDS experience has demonstrated that poor countries can make complex treatments accessible to many people. Regimens that are much simpler to administer than anti-retroviral drugs—like antibiotics for respiratory illnesses, oral rehydration for diarrhea, immunizations and contraception—could also be made widely available. But as there isn't a "global fund" for safe water, child survival and family planning, countries like Senegal—and even poorer ones—cannot directly tackle their real problems without pegging them to the big three diseases.

To their credit, some AIDS advocates are calling for a broader approach to international health programs. Among the presidential candidates, Senator Barack Obama, for example, proposes to go beyond spending for AIDS, tuberculosis and malaria, highlighting the need to also strengthen basic health systems. And recently, Mr. Bush's plan, along with the Global Fund, has become somewhat more flexible in supporting other health issues linked to H.I.V.—though this will be of little use to people, especially outside the "focus" countries, who are dying of common illnesses like diarrhea.

But it is also important, especially for the United States, the world's largest donor, to re-examine the epidemiological and moral foundations of its global health priorities. With 10 million children and a half million mothers in developing countries dying annually of largely preventable conditions, should we mutiply AIDS spending while giving only a pittance for initiatives like safe-water projects?

If one were to ask the people of virtually any African village (outside some 10 countries devastated by AIDS) what their greatest concerns are, the answer would undoubtedly be the less sensational but more ubiquitous ravages of hunger, dirty water and environmental devastation. The real-world needs of Africans struggling to survive should not continue to be subsumed by the favorite causes du jour of well-meaning yet often uninformed Western donors.

7

The Fight Against AIDS Could Be Won with More Government Money

Steve Maich

Steve Maich is a writer for Maclean's *magazine, a Canadian weekly news magazine.*

The financial industry should take an interest in the global economic toll of AIDS. The AIDS epidemic results in slower economic growth in the developing world, which affects economies globally. It would be better to pay up front now to halt the epidemic rather than pay the long-term economic price. Education and prevention take too long, but government spending can do much to help fight AIDS now. Rather than taking over the patented drug formulas of private pharmaceutical companies, governments should fund an initiative to bring HIV/AIDS drugs to the developing world.

Most economists aren't terribly interested in delving into the nitty-gritty of the human condition. They generally prefer to hover in a low orbit, translating massive trends into neat mathematical equations—safe and bloodless and usually pretty dull.

So, last week [August 8, 2006], when TD Economics released a report entitled *The Economic Cost of AIDS: A Clear Case For Action*, you couldn't help but take notice, for the source as much as the subject matter. But TD isn't your typi-

Steve Maich, "A Business Case for Fighting AIDS," *Maclean's*, vol. 119, August 28, 2006, p. 42. Copyright © 2006 by Maclean's Magazine. Reproduced by permission.

cal big bank, and the timing of the report was no coincidence. TD is a main sponsor of the mammoth International AIDS Conference taking place this week in Toronto.

The Economic Effects of AIDS

Laudable though the report is, however, it's unlikely to find much of an audience among the bank's usual clients on Bay Street [Canada's Wall Street]. And that's too bad, because if the suits bothered to crack it, they'd find a compelling argument for immediate and drastic action to fight AIDS—not just because it's morally right, but for reasons that any hard-nosed businessman can appreciate: because, over the long term, the costs of inaction far outweigh the costs of eradicating the disease. "Pay now, or pay a LOT more later," the TD report says.

A few interesting facts that help put the problem in perspective: spending on HIV/AIDS prevention and treatment in the developing world amounts to about US$8 billion a year. By way of comparison, the U.S. spends $17.3 billion domestically each year to fight the disease at home. About 4.1 million people were newly infected last year, 89 per cent of them in sub-Saharan Africa and Asia. As of 2005, only about 10 to 20 per cent of people in low and middle-income countries who need antiretroviral drugs were receiving them. So, while rich countries have slowed the spread of AIDS to a crawl and vastly improved the lives of patients, the disease continues to tear a wide swath through the rest of the world.

AIDS trims as much as one percentage point off of economic growth in the developing world each year.

The World Bank and other agencies have long stuck to the estimate that AIDS trims as much as one percentage point off of economic growth in the developing world each year— which suggests the disease costs the economies of sub-Saharan

Africa about US$6 billion a year. But TD senior economist Beata Caranci, one of the contributors to the report, says that estimate massively underestimates the true toll because it fails to take into account the devastating ripple effect of losing millions of individuals from the labour force every year, and doesn't address massive "informal economies" (black markets and barter trade) common in the Third World.

It's hard to put a dollar figure on the damage, but AIDS is clearly more than just a persistent drag on the economy, as has long been assumed. For example, over the past 30 years, Africa has gone from being a substantial agricultural exporter to a net importer of food. The region can literally no longer feed itself, and AIDS is a major reason why. In the words of the TD report, "in many poorer nations, AIDS threatens to destroy their economic, social and political fabric."

The business case is clear once you take into account the long-term health savings and the benefits of helping turn failed states into contributing members of the world economy.

A Need for Government Investment

So what to do? TD falls back on the same prescriptions we've been hearing for years: a clearer understanding of the problem, and more spending, particularly in the areas of education and prevention. That's all fine, but any field worker can tell you progress on such education campaigns is maddeningly slow.

Health activists usually demand that governments bust patent protections, grab the drug formulas that took many years and millions of dollars to develop by private investors, and churn out generic copies. In other words, screw the drug companies. But doing so would not only offend the whole notion of intellectual property rights, it would kill the incentive for further research into newer and better AIDS drugs. More-over, there's no need to raid the drug makers in order to fight AIDS.

As you may have read in the last issue of *Maclean's*, a group of influential doctors including Dr. Julio Montaner, head of the B.C. Centre for Excellence in HIV/AIDS, is calling on world governments to underwrite a massive effort to get affordable drugs into the hands of all the world's HIV patients—not only to prolong lives and ease suffering, but because antiviral treatment dramatically reduces the chances of further transmission. For years we've been told this is simply unaffordable, but in July of this year the U.S. Food and Drug Administration approved a new once-a-day AIDS drug called Atripla, which will be sold in the developing world for about US$50 a month.

That implies that the 31.4 million AIDS patients in the world's poorest nations could be supplied with drugs at a cost of less than US$20 billion a year. It sounds like a lot of money until you consider that such an effort could make it possible to eradicate AIDS entirely, within our children's lifetime, simply by making the virus more difficult to transmit. Of course, there would be education, administration and distribution costs, plus other drugs needed to fight infections. But the business case is clear once you take into account the long-term health savings and the benefits of helping turn failed states into contributing members of the world economy, rather than breeding grounds of desperation and resentment. As the TD report says, "rather than seeing this as humanitarian aid driven only by altruistic motives [governments] should see it for what it is: a necessary investment in the future economic well-being and security of the industrialized world."

Even economists can't stand back and view AIDS from a safe distance anymore. It is *our* problem, and it's bigger than we think. We have the tools and the money to solve it. All we need now is the will.

8

Charity, Not More Government Money, Should Fund the Fight Against AIDS

Jim DeMint

Jim DeMint is a Republican senator from South Carolina, elected in 2004.

The President's Emergency Plan for AIDS Relief, known as PEP-FAR, began in 2003 with a commitment to abstinence programs. The 2008 proposed reauthorization calling for increased spending and programs not committed to teaching abstinence is unwarranted. The United States faces a huge deficit and cannot afford to adequately fund domestic programs, such as Medicare, as it is. There is not enough money for the government to take care of all problems abroad and, in the case of AIDS, the government should allow Americans to choose what they want to support through their own charitable giving.

Editor's Note: The Tom Lantos and Henry J. Hyde United States Global Leadership Against HIV/AIDS, Tuberculosis and Malaria Reauthorization Act of 2008 passed in July 2008, authorizing increased spending to $48 billion for the five-year period from 2009 to 2013.

America is the greatest nation in the world. Yet, our future is uncertain. We face deficits as far as the eye can see and we are staring down the barrel of a looming entitlement crisis that threatens to bankrupt our country. Indeed, if action is not taken soon, we will reach a tipping point in our two major entitlement programs—Social Security and Medicare—in which the programs will pay out more money than they take in. Our national debt is more than $9 trillion and still Washington will spend $25,117 per household in 2008. We must admit we are a nation pressed to its fiscal limit.

It is against this backdrop that we hear renewed demands for immediate passage of the President's Emergency Plan for AIDS Relief in Africa (PEPFAR). PEPFAR currently weighs in at $50 billion, more than three times President [George W.] Bush's original 2003 proposal. To put this number in perspective, it is more than double the $22 billion we spend each year for our veterans. Meanwhile, back home the federal government cannot even pay doctors what they are owed under Medicare.

When considering PEPFAR we must think hard about our priorities.

This legislation also allows funding for programs that are counterproductive in the fight against AIDS.

Unlike the president's original 2003 legislation, which has been a significant success, this bill allows American dollars to fund programs that teach drug addicts how to inject safely, and prostitutes and homosexuals how to have safe sex. Aside from these practices being morally objectionable to many American taxpayers, they have proven ineffective. According to a recent Harvard School of Public Health Study, such programs have "limited impact" in curtailing the epidemic. The study argues that "reducing multiple sexual partnerships would have a greater impact on the AIDS pandemic and should become the cornerstone of HIV prevention efforts" in Africa. In short, PEPFAR's original commitment to abstinence programs in Africa was on the mark. The new bill misses that mark while tripling the funding.

It must be noted that the increasing calls for immediate passage of PEPFAR contain a distinct whiff of moral superiority. They accuse those of us concerned about America's fiscal collapse and PEPFAR's efficiency of cold-hearted indifference to the plight of our fellow human beings in Africa.

Far from being indifferent to human anguish, we are acutely aware that many Africans suffer pain and hardship as a result of the pandemic.

Though no one has a cure for AIDS, the United States is specially endowed with resources that can, at the margins, alleviate suffering.

A truly compassionate PEPFAR program will find a way to both help AIDS victims in Africa and be fiscally responsible at home.

I have supported, and continue to support, relief efforts that are well designed to assist Africans in this dark moment. However, because the best intentions do not always lead to the best results, I have an obligation to ensure that taxpayer dollars are used wisely and accomplish the program's intended goal.

For starters, rather than heaping additional tens of billions of dollars on the backs of our grandchildren by spending borrowed money, the president and Congress should seek to reduce spending in other areas to pay for the PEPFAR program. A truly compassionate PEPFAR program will find a way to both help AIDS victims in Africa and be fiscally responsible at home.

Second, Congress has a responsibility to the American taxpayer to ensure that aid to Africa is spent effectively. Besides spending money on ineffective programs, the PEPFAR bill actually sends American tax dollars to China and Russia—two countries that both enjoy budget surpluses right now. Until the bill corrects these problems, it does not deserve the blind support that its supporters demand.

Often times, government spending robs the individual from experiencing the personal reward that comes from individual charity.

Third, contrary to the tendencies of the current administration, government spending is not the solution to every problem. There can be a role for federal aid to Africa, but there are other answers as well. No people in the world are more generous with their money than the American people. We have a long and proud tradition of charity in this country.

Just recently the popular TV show "American Idol" raised more than $65 million for aid to Africa and other charities. Before that Americans stunned the world with their generosity in the wake of calamitous tsunamis in Southeast Asia. Indeed, Americans set a record in 2007, giving nearly $300 billion to charity.

When Americans give of their own volition, there is a personal reward for both the giver and the recipient. Often times, government spending robs the individual from experiencing the personal reward that comes from individual charity.

There are enough crises around the world to bankrupt our nation 10 times over. We have a responsibility not to let our hearts run too far ahead of our minds. That said, America can assist Africa, and we can do it responsibly.

The president should call on Congress to trim back PEPFAR funding to his original request and he should bring the plight of the African people before the country. John F. Kennedy once suggested that Americans "ask not what your country can do for you, ask what you can do for your country." In similar fashion, Mr. Bush has an historic opportunity to lead a national charity drive to help our friends in Africa. Ask Americans to help their suffering fellow man and they will.

9

Money Should Be Spent on Testing and Drugs, Not an AIDS Vaccine

Homayoon Khanlou, Michael Weinstein and Lori Yeghiayan

The following article has been reprinted with permission of the authors Homayoon Khanlou, M.D., Chief of Medicine/USA at the AIDS Healthcare Foundation, Michael Weinstein, president and co-founder of the AIDS Healthcare Foundation and Lori Yeghiayan, associate director of communications for the AIDS Healthcare Foundation. The article first appeared in The Baltimore Sun *on March 23, 2008 under the title: "Enough Is Enough: Instead of Continuing to Squander Hundreds of Millions of Dollars on a Futile Quest for an HIV Vaccine, Focus AIDS Spending on Prevention, Testing and Treatment." Founded in 1987, the AIDS Healthcare Foundation (AHF) is the U.S.'s largest nonprofit HIV/AIDS healthcare provider. AHF provides medical care and/or services to more than 100,000 individuals in 21 countries worldwide in the U.S., Africa, Latin America/Caribbean and the Asia Pacific Region. For more information, please visit: www.aidshealth.org.*

After researchers have spent more than twenty years trying to find a vaccine to prevent HIV and AIDS, there are no signs that a vaccine is possible. The millions of dollars being spent on the search for a vaccine would be much better spent on prevention, *testing, and treatment. More money should be spent on routine testing, so that people can know their HIV status and get treatment if necessary. The best way to halt the spread of HIV is to spend money on universal access to antiretroviral treatment, which would drastically slow the spread of HIV and reduce the number of AIDS deaths.*

To control AIDS, funding must be invested in strategies that work: effective prevention efforts, routine testing and universal access to treatment and not spent on expensive vaccine research that over 20 years has yielded little of promise other than discovering how not to make an AIDS vaccine.

No Vaccine for HIV/AIDS

The latest round of vaccine trial failures (including a large-scale Merck trial halted when the vaccine turned out to have possibly increased subjects' risk of acquiring HIV) has added to a growing consensus in the scientific community that an AIDS vaccine is a decade or more away, if one can be developed at all.

Dr. Anthony S. Fauci, director of the National Institute of Allergy and Infectious Diseases, recently stated: "We have to leave open the possibility that we might never get a vaccine for HIV." That view was shared by leading AIDS expert David Baltimore, who conceded last month [February 2008] that the scientific community is no closer now to discovering an HIV vaccine than it was 20 years ago.

It is highly unlikely that there will be an AIDS vaccine.

Twenty years of research and the fact remains: A vaccine against a retrovirus, the family of viruses HIV belongs to, has never been successfully developed. It is highly unlikely that there will be an AIDS vaccine certainly not by any current definition of the word.

Despite this record of failure, the U.S. budget for HIV vaccine research continues to increase, more than doubling between 2000 and 2006 from $327 million to $854 million.

Meanwhile, funding for HIV/AIDS care in the U.S. has flat-lined. And around the world, millions are dying for lack of access to a 5-cent condom, a $15 HIV test or antiretroviral therapy costing as little as 50 cents a day.

It is time to stop the waste.

The Need for More Testing

We already know what a successful AIDS control program looks like: effective prevention, routine testing and access to treatment. Government funding of AIDS vaccine research should be ended and this money put to more productive, and life-saving, uses. If funding being poured into HIV vaccine research were applied to these strategies, much could be achieved.

Achieving universal access to treatment would make the most significant contribution to a drop in AIDS deaths and in HIV transmission rates worldwide.

Though undiagnosed HIV infection is responsible for most new cases, routine testing is still far from reality in the United States or abroad. It is estimated that one-quarter of the more than 1 million Americans living with HIV/AIDS are unaware they are infected; if the majority of the 250,000 undiagnosed cases were diagnosed over the next five years, new infections could be reduced by as much as 50 percent.

Likewise for the estimated 20 million people in the world who are HIV-positive but do not know it: Applying $1 billion toward the rapid scale-up of HIV testing worldwide would likely prevent millions of new infections.

Treatment Should Be the Priority

Achieving universal access to treatment would make the most significant contribution to a drop in AIDS deaths and in HIV transmission rates worldwide.

Largely because of programs such as PEPFAR (the President's Emergency Plan for AIDS Relief), 2 million people in the developing world are receiving treatment, a tremendous feat. However, this is only a small fraction of those who need it and who will die without it. A billion dollars a year in U.S. vaccine funding will do nothing to prevent that.

Bolstering the case for increasing access to treatment is a recent study conducted by the U.S. Centers for Disease Control and Prevention indicating that AIDS drugs render an HIV-positive person significantly less infectious. The study of married couples, conducted over three years in Uganda, assessed the long-term effect of antiretroviral treatment on HIV transmission. Results demonstrate up to a 90 percent reduction in the likelihood that an HIV-positive husband will infect his partner if he is receiving prevention counseling services and antiretroviral drug treatment.

Inhibiting the virus' ability to replicate, antiretroviral drugs lower what is known as the viral load in a person's system, often to such a degree that the virus, while not eliminated, becomes undetectable. Scale-up of treatment worldwide must be our highest priority.

Suspending U.S. funding for an HIV vaccine and investing in strategies that save lives and stop new infections is the wisest and most effective use of limited public resources. And with thousands of lives lost daily because people around the world lack access to proven, effective and relatively inexpensive prevention and treatment options, it is also the only moral choice.

10

A Vaccine Is a Critical Tool to Fighting AIDS Worldwide

Mark Mulligan, James Curran, Eric Hunter, and Carlos del Rio

Mark Mulligan is executive director of the Hope Clinic of the Emory Vaccine Center at Emory University School of Medicine. James Curran is dean of the Rollins School of Public Health at Emory University and co-director of the Emory Center for AIDS Research. Eric Hunter is a professor of pathology and laboratory medicine at Emory University, and co-director of the Emory Center for AIDS Research. Carlos del Rio is a professor of medicine at Emory University and co-director of the Emory Center for AIDS Research.

Although funds for prevention, testing, and treatment of HIV/AIDS need to be increased, this should not come at the expense of research into an HIV vaccine. New HIV infections cannot be adequately prevented without developing an HIV vaccine. Though research has not yielded an HIV vaccine after twenty years, this is not a reason to stop funding the research. History shows that vaccines can take time to develop—the polio vaccine took longer than twenty years to be successful. Funding for an HIV vaccine should continue and possibly be increased.

Drs. Homayoon Khanlou and Michael Weinstein of the AIDS Healthcare Foundation made several statements with which we strongly disagree.

Mark Mulligan, James Curran, Eric Hunter, and Carlos del Rio, "Vaccine Search Is Vital in HIV/AIDS Arsenal," *Atlanta Journal-Constitution*, April 10, 2008. Reproduced by permission of the authors.

Global access to HIV/AIDS prevention, testing and antiretroviral treatment is inadequate, and increased funding is needed. We strongly disagree, however, with the suggestion by Khanlou and Weinstein that the best way to fight AIDS is to end government funding for HIV vaccine research and to redirect those funds to prevention, testing and treatment.

Treatment Can Only Do So Much

History teaches that it is wrong to take an either/or approach to the provision of health care services and vaccine research. In the U.S., despite sustained prevention efforts and widespread use of antiretroviral treatment, 40,000 people are infected with HIV each year. Globally, more than 33 million are infected with HIV. UNAIDS [Joint United Nations Programme on HIV/AIDS] estimates that in 2007, 2.5 million people became infected and 2.1 million deaths occurred from AIDS. Each day, 6,800 persons become infected and 5,700 die from AIDS.

The world desperately needs a vaccine for HIV prevention.

Despite impressive initial steps in antiretroviral rollout in developing countries—due to the U.S. President's Emergency Plan for AIDS Relief [PEPFAR] and other programs—only a fraction of those in need of treatment have received it. The number of HIV-infected persons being treated with antiretroviral drugs in less developed countries is fewer than either the number of deaths or new infections in a single year. Since therapy does not cure HIV, every new infection represents a person who ultimately must be treated for life.

More attention to HIV prevention is urgently needed, and quality education, counseling and testing and other services are warranted. Even when these are fully utilized, it is likely that the number of new infections will remain high.

Vaccines Take Time

New and better HIV prevention interventions are clearly required. Historically, vaccines have been the most effective weapons against infectious diseases. The world desperately needs a vaccine for HIV prevention. Khanlou and Weinstein incorrectly stated that there is no precedent for a vaccine against the retroviruses, the viral family to which HIV belongs. Veterinarians administer a vaccine for protection against the leading viral killer of cats, a retrovirus called feline leukemia virus.

Research is a time-consuming process of trial and error, hypothesis generation and testing, refinement and retesting. Vaccine development historically has taken decades, with each interim result contributing new knowledge. The recent clinical trial called the Step Study tested one candidate HIV vaccine. It was disappointing that the vaccine did not protect those who received it. But the study was successful in that it was well-executed and efficiently provided an answer, albeit not the desired one.

History provides powerful lessons. The virus that causes polio was discovered in the 1930s. Initial vaccines tested in the 1930s were ineffective. In the 1940s and early 1950s, summertime polio epidemics caused fear and panic in industrialized countries. Fortunately, vaccine research continued despite initial failures. Progress was based on incremental scientific advances such as the discovery in 1949 by John Enders and his colleagues of how to grow the polio virus in the laboratory. Six years later Jonas Salk's inactivated, injected polio vaccine became available.

Funding for HIV vaccine research must not be cut.

By 1957, the number of new polio cases annually had fallen by 90 percent, and over time—thanks to sustained scientific effort even in the face of early failures—the iron lung became a museum relic. Imagine if the polio vaccine developers had given up after 20 years, or after a couple of failed vaccine trials.

The National Institutes of Health Summit on HIV Vaccine Research and Development was held in Washington on March 25, [2008] led by Dr. Anthony Fauci, director of the National Institute of Allergy and Infectious Diseases [NIAID]. At this meeting of vaccine and AIDS scientists, care providers and community members, Fauci unequivocally expressed the government's commitment to sustained HIV vaccine research. Based on the input of the summit participants, NIAID will review the balance of resources devoted to HIV/AIDS research and make adjustments to match the state of the science.

Funding for HIV vaccine research must not be cut. If anything, it needs to be increased. Persistence, sustained scientific effort and increased collaboration will drive the quest for an HIV vaccine forward—just as they did for the polio vaccine.

11

The AIDS Epidemic Can Be Controlled While Pursuing a Vaccine

William Haseltine

William Haseltine is the chairman and CEO of Haseltine Associates Ltd. and president of the Haseltine Foundation for Medical Sciences and the Arts, a foundation that supports access to high quality health for the poor and middle class of developing countries, and that also fosters a dialog between sciences and the arts.

Despite the lack of an HIV/AIDS vaccine at the moment, the epidemic can be controlled while a vaccine is developed. The first thing necessary to control the epidemic is to achieve more widespread HIV testing, especially in high-risk areas and in high-risk populations, so that everyone who is infected knows their status. Second, all those who are infected should be treated with a combination of anti-HIV drugs, in order to prolong life and reduce the possibility of transmission. Research to find an HIV/AIDS vaccine should be continued while implementing these control measures.

Preliminary reports on [President Barack] Obama's first budget, to be unveiled tomorrow [February 26, 2009], suggest that funding for international AIDS programs will be held flat, despite campaign-trail promises to ramp up U.S. commitment. Yet now more than ever, investment in the cause can make a difference.

William Haseltine, "An Early End to the HIV/AIDS Pandemic?" *Atlantic Online*, February 25, 2009. Reproduced by permission of the author.

Earlier this week, I met with three colleagues—Robert Gallo, Max Essex, and Robert Redfield—who have been at the forefront of AIDS research for the last 25 years. It was the four of us who in the early '80s helped define the viral nature of the disease, developed the basis for the first diagnostic test, and established a fundamental understanding of the virus, which led directly to the development of effective treatments. We hadn't been together in one place in about a decade, and as we got to talking at Bob Gallo's Institute of Human Virology in Baltimore, we realized we shared a surprising conclusion: The tools to end the AIDS epidemic may well be at hand.

Epidemic control begins with knowing who is infected, so the first step is to detect all those who carry the virus.

Two Steps to Control the Epidemic

Paradoxically, this realization emerges at a low point in our hopes for an HIV/AIDS vaccine. The dramatic failure of the most-promising-seeming vaccine last year dashed such prospects, and sent the community of researchers back to the laboratory. Nevertheless, the epidemic could still be arrested or substantially slowed using diagnostic tests and anti-viral drugs already in existence—saving tens of millions of lives worldwide.

Epidemic control begins with knowing who is infected, so the first step is to detect all those who carry the virus. The means to monitor the progress of the disease are widely available. Reliable, inexpensive diagnostic tests exist and are being used in rich and poor countries alike. And thanks to anti-discrimination policies and the availability of effective, affordable treatments, barriers to testing are falling. In some regions, such as southern Africa, where infection rates exceed 25 percent of the adult population, testing of everyone between the ages of fifteen and fifty might be recommended. Elsewhere, as in the United States and Western Europe, testing could be more focused.

The second step is to treat all those infected with combinations of anti-HIV drugs. Advances in this area have been nothing short of spectacular. More than twenty-five new drugs are currently available, and still more are in the pipeline. When I began my work, HIV infections were almost always fatal. Today, most of those infected with HIV, if carefully treated, can expect to live many decades in relatively good health. Although it is too early to know for sure, it seems likely that the majority of those carrying the virus can expect a normal lifespan.

The Progress of Drug Treatment

The effectiveness of the first therapies was limited by the rapid emergence of viruses within each patient that were resistant to a single drug. The solution was to develop *sets* of drugs, each acting on a different part of the virus. At present, drugs that inhibit six different steps required for virus growth are available. Using combinations of these drugs greatly slows the development of drug resistance. And when resistant viruses do emerge, different combinations of these drugs are often effective. Such progress is a triumph of modern medical science.

Initially, effective HIV/AIDS treatments were available only to those living in wealthy countries. The cost of drug therapy ranged from $10,000 to $15,000 dollars a year in rich and poor countries alike. Today, combination therapy is available in some countries for as little as $75 a year. And agencies such as the Global Fund [to Fight AIDS, Tuberculosis and Malaria] and the U.S.-sponsored PEPFAR [President's Emergency Plan for AIDS Relief] program provide drug treatment free of charge to many less developed countries. Thanks to this dramatic reduction in cost, more than 3 million people in poorer countries are currently receiving treatment through these and other programs. With continued support, that number will grow.

Despite such progress, however, the epidemic is outrunning treatment. The World Health Organization [WHO] estimates that there are now about 35 million people infected with HIV, the great majority of them living in sub-Saharan Africa and South Asia. It is also estimated that 2 to 3 million new people are infected with HIV each year. Thus, an effective method for preventing new infections is badly needed, which is why the failure of the HIV/AIDS vaccine trials was so tragic.

It has been found that anti-HIV/AIDS drugs reduce the spread of the virus in several circumstances.

Limiting Transmission by Treatment

In the near term, our hope for preventing new infections arises from recent observations regarding the effectiveness of diagnosis and treatment in limiting transmission: It has been found that anti-HIV/AIDS drugs reduce the spread of the virus in several circumstances. About one third of children born to infected mothers become infected with HIV. In some instances, this transmission occurs before birth, in other instances, during birth trauma. Still others are infected through breast feeding. But evidence suggests that treating the mother with anti-HIV/AIDS drugs can dramatically reduce all three types of transmission.

Preliminary studies by Max Essex, working with a team at Harvard and in Botswana, seem to show that infection of newborns falls to undetectable rates if mothers are treated with combination therapy for the six months before and after birth, providing that the child is weaned at six months. If transmission by such intimate contact as mother to child can be reduced to near zero, it seems likely that other forms of transmission can also be reduced. Several additional studies document the effectiveness of treatment in substantially reducing sexual transmission of the virus in both heterosexual and homosexual couples. Effective treatment may even reduce infections that occur via blood directly, either by transfusion or by sharing blood-contaminated needles.

How does anti-viral therapy work to reduce transmission? The ability of a person to transmit the HIV virus to another through sex or blood, or from mother to child is correlated with the amount of virus in the body—the higher the concentration of the virus, the more efficient the transmission. Effective anti-viral treatments reduce the amount of virus in the body, thereby diminishing the likelihood of transmission: the more complete the viral suppression, the lower the odds of transmission. To summarize, not only does treatment with anti-HIV drugs prolong life, it also reduces, or may in some cases eliminate, the spread of the virus from one person to another.

Both the fundamental and practical studies needed to create an effective HIV/AIDS vaccine should be accelerated.

Controlling the Epidemic

History has shown that epidemics *can* be controlled, even in the absence of a vaccine. Both syphilis and tuberculosis were pandemic at the end of the nineteenth century, and both epidemics were controlled by effective diagnosis and treatment. So, too, might the current HIV/AIDS pandemic be slowed until vaccines are someday available.

I recommend that WHO, PEPFAR and the Global Fund begin studies to assess the effectiveness of universal testing and early treatment for the prevention of HIV transmission. The joint collaboration between Harvard Medical School and the Government of Botswana, now in the advanced planning stages, is one such study. Others should follow soon.

Meanwhile, we should also continue our efforts to control the epidemic via other means: both the fundamental and practical studies needed to create an effective HIV/AIDS vaccine should be accelerated; countries and regions should increase their efforts to promote condoms and educate the public regarding the risks of infection; and programs to encourage male circumcision, shown to reduce the risk of HIV infection, should also be implemented where appropriate.

But the continued and rapid spread of HIV infection demonstrates that such measures are not sufficient to stop the epidemic. Something more is needed. I believe that our best hope now lies in universal detection and universal treatment of all those currently HIV positive. It is time to begin. We cannot afford to wait.

12

Strategies to Prevent AIDS Should Emphasize Abstinence

Edward C. Green

Edward C. Green, a medical anthropologist and senior research scientist at the Harvard Center for Population and Development Studies, was a member of the Presidential Advisory Committee on HIV/AIDS, and also served on the National Institutes of Health's AIDS advisory council, OARAC. He is the author of Rethinking AIDS Prevention: Learning from Successes in Developing Countries.

Uganda reduced the level of HIV infection between 1991 and 2004 by using an unpopular prevention approach. Its approach was to promote abstinence among unmarried people and encourage fidelity among the married, with condoms only relevant for a small part of the population. The Western view that promotion of abstinence and fidelity will not work in Africa is condescending in its view of Africans as too hypersexed for such an approach. In fact, the approach worked well until Western donors started insisting on an HIV-prevention model that promotes condoms. Ideology and profit motives need to be abandoned in favor of this low-cost prevention model that works.

For many years, there was an open secret in the battle against AIDS in Africa. A few of us knew about, and earnestly sought to publicize, crucial findings indicating the most effective approach to AIDS prevention. Yet the "experts" in the

Edward C. Green, "Imposing Western Solutions on AIDS in Africa," *Weekly Standard*, vol. 10, January 31, 2005, pp. 27–29. Copyright © 2005 News Corporation, *Weekly Standard*. All rights reserved. Reproduced by permission of the author.

field didn't want to hear. Our secret was that the country that had best succeeded in curbing the spread of HIV—Uganda—had achieved this result without following the formula the experts had been pushing for over 20 years, namely, condoms, drugs, and testing. Instead, Uganda had achieved its unparalleled decline in the prevalence of HIV with a home-grown, low-cost program built around something offensive to conventional experts: promotion of sexual abstinence and fidelity, with condoms promoted only quietly, to high-risk groups and those already infected.

Evidence in Uganda

The figures are startling. Through a public-information campaign backed by local medical personnel, pastors, and imams and reinforced in schools, Uganda reduced its HIV rate from 15 percent to 4 percent between 1991 and 2004, according to a U.N. [United Nations] calculation.

> *How infuriating that an approach not funded by the big donors and scoffed at by foreign experts should prove to be the very thing that worked best.*

Not surprisingly, information about what was actually working in Uganda was unpopular. Condoms have been regarded as the first line of defense for everyone, everywhere, and anyone who disagrees with this orthodoxy has been dismissed as a religious fanatic with "an agenda." Hundreds of millions of dollars have been spent on condom social marketing (a field I myself worked in for several years) and on related medical-pharmaceutical solutions. How infuriating that an approach not funded by the big donors and scoffed at by foreign experts should prove to be the very thing that worked best.

Abstinence and fidelity, of course, are precisely what religious conservatives have always argued for, and partly for this reason predominantly secular or liberal AIDS experts dismissed the possibility that they might work. For the fact is, as I learned during my lonely battle to broadcast the truth about Uganda, abstinence and fidelity challenge core values and attitudes enshrined by the Western sexual revolution, which taught that people, whether straight or gay, have the right to express their sexuality however they wish, as long as all participants are consenting adults and no one is hurt. Finally, few AIDS experts wanted to accept the evidence from Uganda because people do not like to admit they might have been wrong, especially in a matter involving countless millions of dollars and the lives of millions of people.

The Condescending Critics' View

Consider this vignette, from the global AIDS conference in Bangkok in July 2004. When Simon Onaba, a 22-year-old Ugandan university student, told an audience of AIDS experts that he had abstained from sex for three years and intended to continue doing so until his wedding night, he was loudly jeered. "Oh, how nice for you!" went one reaction. "You may be able to abstain, but what about a 13-year-old Somali girl forced into marriage and subjected to genital mutilation? She doesn't have the luxury to abstain!" (As if, by choosing abstinence, Simon were somehow failing to take a stand against genital mutilation.) The experts also hurled hostile questions at Simon: How often do you masturbate, and with whom? What's your real agenda for trying to make people believe you are abstaining?

These critics seem to believe that since abstinence and fidelity may not be workable options for 5 percent of the population, they should be rejected altogether, even if they are the best option for 95 percent of the population. These numbers are not arbitrary: By 1995, only 5 percent of Ugandan males and females were reporting casual sex.

As that last figure suggests, reality is very different from the Western experts' perception. Surveys today suggest that more than half of African males and females between the ages of 15 and 19 are abstaining from premarital sex, and increasing proportions of adults are having sex with only one partner. Yet few who work in AIDS prevention have called attention to these important trends, perhaps because they contradict the image of the hypersexed African that Western AIDS experts have been selling since the beginning of the AIDS pandemic. They depict Africans as "polygamous by nature," and supposedly so driven by hormones and poverty that commercial and transactional sex, and the inability to make responsible decisions about sex, are simply part of what it means to be African. If you accept this condescending view, condoms seem to be the only realistic solution to AIDS.

Not only in Uganda, but also perhaps in Senegal, Kenya, and elsewhere, abstinence and faithfulness have worked better than condoms.

The ABC Approach

The trouble with the image of the hypersexed African is that it was never true for most Africans. Meanwhile, sexual behavior in Africa has changed. Not only in Uganda, but also perhaps in Senegal, Kenya, and elsewhere, abstinence and faithfulness have worked better than condoms. I document the evidence for Uganda and Senegal in detail in my 2003 book *Rethinking AIDS Prevention.* I also show that in about 1999, Kenya switched to a Uganda-style approach. In the past four to five years, casual sex on the part of Kenyan men and women has declined by about 50 percent, and HIV infection rates have fallen.

The prevention component of President [George W.] Bush's Emergency Plan for AIDS Relief is based on Uganda's "ABC" model: Abstain, Be faithful, or use a Condom, with condoms the last line of defense. When Congress passed the United States Leadership Against HIV/AIDS, Tuberculosis, and Malaria Act of 2003, it stipulated that a third of all prevention money appropriated under the bill be spent on abstinence programs. The law also allowed faith-based organizations to be funded by the U.S. government for AIDS-prevention without being *required* to promote condoms.

Reactions to these provisions in the professional AIDS community were immediate and highly emotional. There were predictions of mass death, since a dollar spent on abstinence meant a dollar less for condoms. The drumbeat for condoms continued, even though at about the same time a U.N. AIDS report concluded, "There are no definite examples yet of generalized epidemics that have been turned back by prevention programs based primarily on condom promotion." The U.S. Agency for International Development [USAID] itself published a study in 2003 showing that HIV infection rates in "generalized epidemics" simply do not decline unless there are "A and B" behavioral changes—that is, increases in abstinence and fidelity.

An Overfocus on Condoms

Now, more than a year after the administration's AIDS program became law, one would expect the ABC model to have been replicated around the world. Sadly, it is not so. Instead, even in its country of origin, the model has fallen into disrepair.

Relentlessly pressed by Western donors including USAID to favor condoms, Uganda has started to abandon its highly effective "Be faithful" intervention strategy.

Visitors to Uganda in recent years have found an AIDS-prevention program that looks more and more like that of any other country in Africa: condom social marketing, supplemented by treatment of sexually transmitted diseases, testing, and provision of nevirapine to pregnant mothers. Relentlessly pressed by Western donors including USAID to favor condoms, Uganda has started to abandon its highly effective "Be faithful" intervention strategy. A USAID officer in Uganda admitted to me (in front of the U.S. ambassador, in November 2004) that there are currently no plans for interventions that promote fidelity or partner reduction. I wrote three follow-up letters to the U.S. ambassador providing evidence that Uganda's ABC model "has been diluted and marginalized since the early '90s, largely because the international donors have exclusively or primarily promoted 'risk reduction' (condom) interventions, and have not put actual resources into abstinence/delay or faithfulness/partner-reduction interventions." (The U.S. ambassador is the head of the Bush AIDS-relief team in every participating country.) My letters went unanswered.

Already in December 2002, when I was part of a delegation that visited Uganda, we sat through a two-hour presentation by staff of USAID and the Centers for Disease Control and Prevention stationed in Uganda. The title of the presentation was "What Happened in Uganda?" Not once did these American government personnel mention abstinence or faithfulness, or even partner-reduction or the decline in casual sex. They spoke exclusively about latex, drugs, vaccine research, and hopes for more medical products in the future.

Last summer I was back in Uganda. Conspicuously missing from the national AIDS strategy and other planning documents was any sign of A or B interventions. Not missing was C: Condom initiatives were plentiful and ubiquitous. Prior to 2001, AIDS planning and policy documents were full of A and B objectives and program indicators. One of the early AIDS-prevention manuals produced by the Ugandan government, Control of AIDS (1989), was mostly about abstinence and faithfulness. Condoms were not even mentioned until page

32, and then the booklet originally cautioned, "The government does not recommend using condoms as a way to fight AIDS." UNICEF [United Nations Children's Fund], which paid for the booklet, was so unhappy with this anti-condom statement that it pasted a new, more pro-condom page 32 over the original one before releasing the booklet.

The Power of Donors

Uganda is a poor country, still rebuilding its economy after the havoc wreaked by two dictators. Like other sub-Saharan nations, Uganda relies heavily on Western aid. Because they pay the bills, foreign donors have a great deal of influence on national strategy, and they have been systematically undermining Uganda's uniquely successful AIDS-prevention model. Indeed, with rare exceptions, they have simply refused to pay for programs that promote abstinence, fidelity, and reduction in the number of sexual partners. This is supposed to change under the 2003 emergency AIDS relief legislation. But change, always slow in coming, is being vigorously resisted by major AIDS donors.

Western donor organizations and many of the groups they support that are doing the work on the ground simply continue to promote condoms and avoid addressing sexual behavior.

A member of the Uganda AIDS Commission, after describing the central role of abstinence and faithfulness in his country's success at controlling the disease, observed to me that messages promoting abstinence and faithfulness "have somehow faded since the early 1990s. We sometimes see faded billboards that used to have AIDS messages. Now they just have messages about condoms." And during a meeting of top religious leaders in Uganda in November 2004, one cleric after another complained that they had become increasingly marginalized, while foreign experts scoffed at abstinence and faithfulness as prevention strategies.

Western donor organizations and many of the groups they support that are doing the work on the ground simply continue to promote condoms and avoid addressing sexual behavior. Even USAID, an agency I have worked under for 25 years, has failed to support adequately the goals of President Bush's plan, often awarding funds earmarked for abstinence to condom social marketing companies (especially in Uganda, of all places). This simply ensures business as usual. Most of the people and organizations who actually implement AIDS-prevention programs do not believe in or support the new ABC policy.

A Strategy in Jeopardy

Senator Sam Brownback [R-Kansas] recently visited Uganda. In his trip report he confirms that Western donors, including the U.S. government, are undermining the once successful ABC model. The vast majority of prevention funds have gone to condoms, Brownback says, and "PSI, a well-known condom social marketing NGO [non-governmental organization], is still the largest U.S.-funded HIV prevention contractor in Uganda." Further, Ugandan president Yoweri Museveni, the original champion of ABC, "is in a battle with Western donors to keep condom promotion out of his innovative AIDS education program in public primary schools, . . . [and] African leaders are growing resentful that U.S. dollars are contingent upon acceptance [of condoms as the main prevention strategy]."

Because of the problems Brownback and I have pointed out, the senator calls for congressional and GAO [Government Accountability Office] oversight over future spending under the Bush AIDS initiative, a cumbersome precaution that could easily have been avoided had USAID (and the Centers for Disease Control) simply had the humility and good sense to allow Uganda to continue an indigenous program that had already proven successful.

Last November [2004], a number of colleagues and I published a statement in the *Lancet* about what works best in preventing sexually transmitted HIV in Africa. It reflects Uganda's ABC prevention strategy in the early years, when sexual behavior changed most dramatically. Some 150 scientists and the president of Uganda endorsed the statement. Unfortunately, it is by no means clear that empirical evidence can overcome ideological blinders or compete with the big business in pharmaceutical products that AIDS prevention has become. As a result, not only the improved AIDS situation in Uganda, but also the integrity of President Bush's entire global AIDS-prevention strategy, are in jeopardy.

Recent Research

Since publication of this paper in 2005, an expanding body of largely recent research has found medical risk reduction (condoms, testing, treating the curable sexually transmitted infections) to be largely ineffective in the African population-wide epidemics. For example, in a 2008 article in *Science* called "Reassessing HIV Prevention," ten AIDS experts concluded that "consistent condom use has not reached a sufficiently high level, even after many years of widespread and often aggressive promotion, to produce a measurable slowing of new infections in the generalized epidemics of Sub-Saharan Africa." They conclude that reduction in multiple and concurrent partners is the key behavior change and intervention in Africa's so called hyper-epidemics. We are now seeing declines in HIV prevalence in several African countries, always preceded by evidence of both men and women reporting fewer sexual partners in the previous year. Fidelity is not just a factor, it is the factor in explaining the rise and fall of HIV epidemics.

In January 2009, the Harvard AIDS Prevention Project, along with UNAIDS [Joint United Nations Programme on HIV/AIDS] and the World Bank, co-hosted a conference on multiple and concurrent partners in Botswana. In April 2009, UNAIDS released a report based on the joint conference, "Addressing Multiple and Concurrent Partnerships in Southern Africa: Developing Guidance for Bold Action."

This must be the first time the UN [United Nations] has placed behavior change (mutual monogamy,) as a higher priority than condom promotion, testing or drugs. In fact, mutual monogamy hasn't been a priority at all. A great deal of bias against any intervention that seems to restrict complete sexual freedom in any way still constrains an evidence-based approach, but the entrenched paradigm is slowly crumbling.

13

Strategies to Prevent AIDS Should Not Emphasize Abstinence

Geraldine Sealey

Geraldine Sealey is the articles editor at Glamour *magazine.*

The global AIDS initiative introduced by President George W. Bush in 2003 has made abstinence the focus of HIV prevention. The emphasis on abstinence is not driven by public health research but, instead, by religious ideology. Focusing on abstinence is not only ineffective in reducing the spread of HIV, it is dangerous in that it results in lowered use of contraception. Religious conservatives wrongly claim that Uganda's lowered HIV infection rate was due to a focus on abstinence and monogamy, and have continued to push a dangerous abstinence-only approach. HIV prevention should be driven by public health concerns and not by religious ideology, as a focus on new methods that do not work will result in unnecessary deaths.

When President [George W.] Bush introduced his global AIDS initiative in January 2003—"a work of mercy beyond all current international efforts," he called it—the plan certainly sounded promising. Bush pledged to spend $15 billion over five years to provide life-saving drugs to at least 2 million people with HIV, prevent 7 million new infections, and care for the sick and orphaned in 15 countries. Most of the money would go to sub-Saharan Africa, home to the ma-

Geraldine Sealey, "An Epidemic Failure," Salon.com, June 2, 2005. This article first appeared in Salon.com, at http://www.salon.com. An online version remains in the Salon archives. Reprinted with permission.

jority of the world's nearly 40 million people living with HIV and AIDS. "I believe God has called us into action," Bush declared during a trip to Uganda in 2003. "We are a great nation. We're a wealthy nation. We have a responsibility to help a neighbor in need, a brother and sister in crisis."

PEPFAR Under Bush

Dubbed the President's Emergency Plan for AIDS Relief, or PEPFAR, the agenda provided the administration with much-needed P.R. [public relations] at the very moment it was preparing to defy international will by invading Iraq. But from the start, Bush has been inexplicably stingy and mind-bogglingly slow to act.

Much of the money Bush has provided is being derailed into moralistic and unproven programs that make abstinence the centerpiece of HIV prevention.

Despite rhetoric about our moral duty to fight AIDS— Bush has likened PEPFAR to the Marshall Plan, the Berlin airlift, and the Peace Corps—the president has not committed the funds necessary to meaningfully tackle the crisis and even opposed attempts in Congress to fully fund his initiative. And much of the money Bush has provided is being derailed into moralistic and unproven programs that make abstinence the centerpiece of HIV prevention. Few Americans realize that the money flowing into disease-ravaged locales is being diverted to serve a right-wing political agenda—at the cost of untold numbers of lives.

Bush requested only $2 billion for PEPFAR in its first year, at least a billion less than one might have expected, given his pledge. Then, when Congress decided to approve $400 million more than the president asked for, Bush unsuccessfully fought to block the increase. By the time the plan was fully implemented, nearly a year and a half had passed since the president had announced it—a costly delay in fighting an epidemic that claims 8,500 lives every day.

As of this month [June 2005], PEPFAR is expected to provide anti-retroviral treatment for an estimated 200,000 people, mainly in sub-Saharan Africa. "I think those numbers are cause for encouragement and optimism," Bush's global AIDS czar, Ambassador Randall Tobias, told me recently. "I think there's reason to believe this can be done." But in a region where 25.4 million people living with HIV are desperate for treatment, it's difficult to feel elated about our progress—or our commitment.

Tobias, a former CEO of Eli Lilly and Co., has found himself under international fire as Bush's AIDS emissary. Last year, Tobias was booed at the International AIDS Conference in Bangkok by protesters carrying signs that read: "He's lying." And as a former pharmaceutical executive, he's taken heat for the administration's insistence on relying on brand-name AIDS drugs instead of generics that are two to four times cheaper. "There comes a moment in time," says Stephen Lewis, the U.N. [United Nations] secretary-general's special envoy for HIV/AIDS in Africa, "when you stop bowing to Big Pharma and recognize that the human imperative at stake of keeping people alive requires that we embrace low-cost generics because we can treat so many more people." Lewis rejects the administration's argument that generics are less safe and effective than brand-name drugs. "Everyone understands that the position which is taken [by the U.S. government] significantly supports major pharmaceutical companies," he said.

Twelve million people died of AIDS in Bush's first term.

Not Enough Money

As it stands, what we're doing barely factors into the disease's devastating arithmetic. Twelve million people died of AIDS in

Bush's first term. "Bush's initiative is going slow," says Dr. Paul Zeitz, executive director of Global AIDS Alliance. "We're not coming near meeting the need or what is possible. If I were Ambassador Tobias, I wouldn't be defending this current framework. I'd be going back to the president and saying: I know we have a role to play. Why not ramp this up so we can stop the dying?"

The truth is, we *are* doing something, but not nearly what we could be doing. Although other priorities dwarf Bush's AIDS program—$136 billion in new corporate tax breaks, for example—the United States is the largest single donor to the global AIDS fight. But it would be a tremendous embarrassment if we weren't: The United States accounts for one-third of the global GDP [gross domestic product].

The administration insists it will meet its goals by 2008, saying it planned all along to gradually "ramp up" the program. This year, the United States is spending $2.8 billion on PEPFAR, and Bush has asked for $3.2 billion in 2006. But public-health experts say it looks increasingly unlikely that Bush will fulfill his promise of $15 billion over five years—and that even if he does, the money will fall far short of what is needed.

According to UNAIDS [Joint United Nations Programme on HIV/AIDS], a partnership involving the World Bank and nine other international aid groups, the world needs to spend $20 billion a year by 2007 to wage an effective war against AIDS. What Bush proposes to spend annually, if funding remains constant, is less than half the $6.6 billion that America would be expected to contribute based on the size of its economy. "The fact that the United States can spend $300 billion on the wars in Iraq and Afghanistan but cannot find a relative pittance to rescue the human condition in Africa—there is something profoundly out of whack about that," Lewis says.

Reinventing the Wheel

The president's AIDS initiative, like his invasion of Iraq, is a go-it-alone affair that ignores the clear global consensus on how to fight AIDS. In launching his own initiative, Bush has shifted the bulk of U.S. money away from the Global Fund to Fight AIDS, Tuberculosis and Malaria, an international financing mechanism established before PEPFAR and widely recognized as the best way to distribute AIDS funds. "Bush is starving the fund," Zeitz says. "It's despicable, frankly."

Unlike PEPFAR, which focuses on 15 countries—inexplicably excluding the AIDS-ravaged nations of Swaziland and Lesotho among others—the Global Fund has committed funds to 128 countries. Economist Jeffrey Sachs, special advisor to U.N. Secretary-General Kofi Annan, recognizes the Bush administration's modus operandi. "This group is so convinced they have to do everything by themselves even though they often know the least about the issue," he said. "They reinvent everything—reinvent it wrong at the beginning, learn along the way, explain that it takes time, and here we are." Where we are, unfortunately, is much like where we were two and half years ago.

Bush is using AIDS funds to place religion over science, promoting abstinence and monogamy over comprehensive sex education that includes information about and access to condoms.

But the failures of Bush's global AIDS policy go beyond how much money is being spent. Perhaps even more disturbing is how it's being spent. Overlooking the grim realities on the ground, Bush is using AIDS funds to place religion over science, promoting abstinence and monogamy over comprehensive sex education that includes information about and access to condoms. This should be no surprise, given the administration's track record. Yet it is still shocking to observe an administration that claims to be acting in the name of morality consigning tens of thousands, perhaps millions, of people to death because of its policies.

The ABC Approach

In 2002, America joined Libya, Sudan, Iran, Iraq and Syria—a veritable axis of the unenlightened—to scuttle an endorsement of sex education from a global declaration on children's health. Before overseas groups can receive U.S. funding, the Bush administration requires them to take a "loyalty oath" to condemn prostitution—a provision that AIDS workers say further stigmatizes a population in need of HIV education and treatment. Brazil recently became the first country to rebel against the oath, announcing in May [2005] that it was rejecting $40 million in AIDS grants from the administration. "What we're doing is imposing a really misguided and ill-informed ideology on top of a public health crisis," says Jodi Jacobson, executive director of the Center for Health and Gender Equity in Takoma Park, Md.

Scientific evidence shows no indication that trying to persuade young people to abstain from sex at the expense of condom education reduces the spread of HIV.

Just as U.S. abstinence-only programs that push partial or false information on teens have doubled under Bush, so are such morality-driven programs cropping up under U.S. auspices in places like Africa—where the stakes are much higher and a lack of vital information can kill. PEPFAR is fast becoming equated with a notorious emphasis on abstinence education—nearly $1 billion of Bush's global AIDS pledge is earmarked for abstinence promotion. Bush's plan calls for an ABC approach to HIV prevention—which stands for "Abstinence, Being faithful, Condom use," but the administration is stressing the "A." In its first year, PEPFAR spent more than half of the $92 million earmarked to prevent sexual transmission on promoting abstinence programs. "It's only a matter of time before the impact of abstinence-only programs can be measured in needless new HIV infections," says Jonathan Cohen, an HIV/AIDS researcher with Human Rights Watch.

The Risks of Focusing on Abstinence

Administration officials deny inappropriately stressing abstinence over all else, and point out that the epidemic worsened in Africa and other nations even with condom promotion. "If there is a sense of focus on abstinence until marriage now, it's because we've never been focused on these important things," said Dr. Mark Dybul, assistant U.S. global AIDS coordinator. But there is a good reason global AIDS experts haven't focused on abstinence: Scientific evidence shows no indication that trying to persuade young people to abstain from sex at the expense of condom education reduces the spread of HIV. Studies show that such programs actually increase risk by discouraging contraceptive use.

What's more, focusing on abstinence and monogamy ignores the reality facing young women and girls in Africa and other impoverished regions, who are often infected by wandering husbands or forced to have sex in exchange for food or shelter. Among 15- to 24-year-olds in sub-Saharan Africa, studies show, more than three times as many young women are infected with HIV as young men. Preaching about abstinence and faithfulness to girls and women in risky situations "can't be made sense of on any level," Jacobson says. "It's not only contrary to public-health best practices, it's contrary to common sense and contrary to human rights principles."

The emphasis on morality is being driven by social conservatives who have made spreading the gospel of abstinence and monogamy to Africans their primary mission. "Condoms promote promiscuity," says Derek Gordon of the evangelical Christian group Focus on the Family. "When you give a teen a condom, it gives them a license to go out and have sex." At a congressional hearing in April, Rep. Henry Hyde, R-Ill., threatened to cut funding for organizations that promote condoms. "The best defense for preventing HIV transmission is practicing abstinence and being mutually faithful to a non-infected partner," Hyde declared. And under a proposal being pushed by Hyde and his Republican colleagues on Capitol Hill, Tobias would be given the power to divert even more money toward promoting abstinence. "All [conservatives] can think about is making Africans abstinent and monogamous," says a Democratic staffer. "It's the crassest form of international social engineering you could imagine."

The Case of Uganda

Nowhere is the effort by conservative Republicans to turn back the clock on sex education more pronounced than in Uganda. By aggressively promoting condom use and sex education, Uganda has managed to cut its HIV rate from 15 percent of the population to barely 6 percent during the past decade, making it Africa's biggest success story. Social conservatives argue that an emphasis on abstinence and monogamy drove down Uganda's HIV prevalence—and if only other African nations could adopt such rigid moral standards, they would see similar success. While it's true that partner reduction may well have helped lower Uganda's HIV rates, the role of abstinence has been distorted and overblown by evangelicals seeking to control U.S. AIDS funds.

Under pressure from the Bush administration, Uganda has taken a dangerous turn toward an abstinence-only approach. In April, the country's Ministry of Education banned the promotion and distribution of condoms in public schools. To make matters worse, the government has even engineered a nationwide shortage of condoms, issuing a recall of all state-supplied condoms and impounding boxes of condoms imported from other countries at the airport, claiming they need to be tested for quality control. As of this year [2005], a top health official announced, the government will "be less involved in condom importation but more involved in awareness campaigns: abstinence and behavior change."

The Bush administration is supporting the shift by pumping $10 million into abstinence-only programs in Uganda. "One can put a dollar figure on the political pressure," says Cohen, who has closely studied the initiatives in Uganda. "Groups know the more they talk about abstinence, the more they'll get U.S. funding. And they fear that if they talk about condoms they'll lose funding—or, worse, get kicked out of the country."

Tobias issued written guidelines to PEPFAR partners in January [2005] that spell out the administration's agenda. Groups that receive U.S. funding, Tobias warned, should not target youth with messages that present abstinence and condoms as "equally viable, alternative choices." Zeitz of Global AIDS Alliance has dubbed the document "Vomitus Maximus." He says, "I get physically ill when I read it. It has the biggest influence over how people are acting in the field."

A Religious Agenda Trumps Public Health

The anti-condom order issued by Tobias is already having a chilling effect among the groups most effective at combating AIDS. Population Services International [PSI], a major U.S. contractor with years of experience in HIV prevention, says it can no longer promote condoms to youth in Uganda, Zambia and Namibia because of PEPFAR rules. "That's worrisome," says PSI spokesman David Olson. "The evidence shows they're having sex. You can disapprove of that, but you can't deny it's happening." What's more, conservatives are attacking PSI for promoting condoms—a campaign that prevented an estimated 800,000 cases of HIV last year. Focus on the Family recently denounced PSI as a "shady" and "sordid" organization that is leading Africans into immorality.

And in April, conservative Republicans in the House invited Martin Ssempa, a Ugandan minister, to Capitol Hill, to berate PSI for "promoting promiscuity and condoms" in his country. "Today, we face a new enemy in the fight against HIV/AIDS, not only in Uganda but in all the other African countries," Ssempa told the House International Relations Committee. "That enemy is the Western belief that condoms can end the HIV/AIDS epidemic." The attacks on PSI have become so extreme and ideological that even some Republicans think they've gone too far: Utah Sen. Orrin Hatch sent a letter to USAID [U.S. Agency for International Development] last month expressing dismay over "inaccurate information" being spread about PSI. Still, this year, U.S. funding for PSI has been reduced for the first time.

Religious conservatives intent on hijacking global AIDS prevention funds are putting heavy pressure on legislators and the Bush administration to strip funding from established public-health organizations like PSI in favor of faith-based groups that promote a moralistic agenda. Some faith-based organizations have long, admirable histories of working in Africa. But soon, even these groups could face a litmus test—if they don't strictly adhere to abstinence promotion, they could lose funding to smaller, more ideological groups. "Throw out the window any public-health test," Jacobson said.

Groups that support the president's religious agenda . . . are beginning to receive money that has traditionally been devoted to more experienced organizations.

Groups that support the president's religious agenda, meanwhile, are beginning to receive money that has traditionally been devoted to more experienced organizations. The Children's AIDS Fund, a well-connected conservative organization, received roughly $10 million last fall to promote abstinence-only programs overseas—even though the group was deemed "not suitable for funding" by an expert review panel. Fresh Ministries, a Florida organization with little experience in tackling AIDS, also received $10 million. "Bush has enacted policies that will redirect millions of dollars away from groups that have experience fighting HIV and AIDS and toward groups that don't but are members of his religious constituency," Cohen says.

A Deadly Game

In the end, say public-health experts, the administration's diversion of funds from tried-and-true HIV-prevention methods is more than a misguided experiment—it's a deadly game of Russian roulette that could mark a calamitous turn in Africa's attempts to get a handle on the AIDS epidemic.

It's hard to imagine how the health crisis could get worse in sub-Saharan Africa, where life expectancies have plummeted below 40 in some nations and more than 12 million children have been orphaned by AIDS. HIV prevalence has been somewhat stable in recent years, but experts are worried that could be disguising the worst phases of the epidemic, with roughly the same number of people getting newly infected with HIV and dying of AIDS. Africa's fight against AIDS is a tragedy that, with all of the resources at our disposal, we could be doing something about—but so far, we're not. "People will look back and say, Why didn't they stop the dying?" Zeitz says. "Why don't we show our compassionate selves? What kind of country are we?"

Organizations to Contact

The editors have compiled the following list of organizations concerned with the issues debated in this book. The descriptions are derived from materials provided by the organizations. All have publications or information available for interested readers. The list was compiled on the date of publication of the present volume; the information provided here may change. Be aware that many organizations take several weeks or longer to respond to inquiries, so allow as much time as possible.

AVERT
4 Brighton Rd., Horsham, West Sussex   RH13 5BA
   United Kingdom
44 (0) 1-403-210202
e-mail: info@avert.org
Web site: www.avert.org

AVERT is an international HIV and AIDS charity based in the United Kingdom, working to prevent HIV and AIDS worldwide. AVERT has HIV and AIDS projects in countries where there is a particularly high rate of infection, such as sub-Saharan Africa, or where there is a rapidly increasing rate of infection such as in India. AVERT provides AIDS education and information through its Web site, including the article, "HIV Prevention Around the World."

William J. Clinton Foundation
55 W 125th St., New York, NY   10027
(212) 348-8882
Web site: www.clintonfoundation.org

The William J. Clinton Foundation focuses on worldwide issues that demand urgent action, solutions, and measurable results. The Clinton HIV/AIDS Initiative (CHAI) works to negotiate lower prices for lifesaving antiretroviral treatment in the developing world and works with governments to improve the national health care systems required to deliver crucial medicines. The foundation publishes information about CHAI, including reports about its access programs.

Global AIDS Alliance Fund

1121 14th St. NW, Suite 200, Washington, DC   20005
(202) 789-0432 • fax: (202) 789-0715
e-mail: info@globalaidsalliancefund.org
Web site: www.globalaidsalliancefund.org

The Global AIDS Alliance Fund was founded to help accelerate an end to global HIV/AIDS and extreme poverty. The Global AIDS Alliance Fund conducts public education and media outreach to raise awareness, and engages in citizen-based advocacy and lobbying to hold government leaders accountable for concrete action. The fund publishes numerous fact sheets, including "Global AIDS Statistics."

Joint United Nations Programme on HIV/AIDS (UNAIDS)

Avenue Appia 20, Geneva 27   1211
  Switzerland
41-22-791-3666 • fax: 41-22-791-4187
e-mail: distribution@unaids.org
Web site: www.unaids.org

UNAIDS is a joint venture of the United Nations (UN) family, bringing together the efforts and resources of ten UN system organizations in the AIDS response. UNAIDS works to help the world prevent new HIV infections, care for people living with HIV, and mitigate the impact of the epidemic. UNAIDS publishes reports, policies, and briefs on the global AIDS epidemic, including the report, "Making the Money Work: UNAIDS Technical Support to Countries."

Oxfam International

226 Causeway St., 5th Fl., Boston, MA   02114-2206
(800) 77-OXFAM • fax: (617) 728-2594

e-mail: info@oxfamamerica.org
Web site: www.oxfam.org

Oxfam International is a confederation of organizations working to end poverty and injustice. Oxfam's Health and Education campaign works directly with people around the word to help them to get better health care, including working directly with people affected by HIV and AIDS. Oxfam publishes numerous reports and press releases, available at its Web site, including the policy paper, "Mitigating the Impact of HIV/AIDS—Mainstreaming in Action."

Student Global AIDS Campaign (SGAC)
1301 Clifton St. NW, Suite 100, Washington, DC 20009
(202) 296-6727 • fax: (202) 296-6728
e-mail: info@fightglobalaids.org
Web site: www.fightglobalaids.org

SGAC is a national movement with more than 85 chapters at high schools, colleges, and universities across the United States committed to bringing an end to HIV and AIDS around the world. SGAC works to educate students about the global AIDS crisis, lobbies politicians and holds rallies, and raises money for and partners with organizations fighting AIDS. SGAC provides news and information about AIDS at its Web site, as well as information on starting a chapter and fundraising.

UK Consortium on AIDS and International Development
Grayston Centre, 28 Charles Sq., London N1 6HT
    United Kingdom
44 (0)20-7324-4780
e-mail: info@aidsconsortium.org.uk
Web site: www.aidsconsortium.org.uk

The UK Consortium on AIDS and International Development works to encourage, initiate, and support collaborative action by civil society to contribute to and influence the global response to HIV and AIDS. The Stop AIDS Campaign is an initiative of the UK Consortium on AIDS and International Development, bringing together more than 80 of the United Kingdom's leading development and HIV and AIDS groups to raise awareness in the United Kingdom about the global HIV/AIDS epidemic. The consortium publishes a number of policy briefings and reports, including the proposal, "HIV and Health Systems Strengthening: Opportunities for Achieving Universal Access by 2010."

United Nations Children's Fund (UNICEF)
125 Maiden Ln., New York, NY   10038
(212) 326-7000 • fax: (212) 887-7465
Web site: www.unicef.org

UNICEF works to help build a world where the rights of every child are realized. UNICEF works to prevent the spread of HIV among young people and helps children and families affected by HIV/AIDS to live their lives with dignity. UNICEF publishes numerous briefing papers, available at its Web site, including "Scaling up Early Infant Diagnosis and Linkages to Care and Treatment."

World Bank
1818 H St. NW, Washington, DC   20433
(202) 473-1000 • fax: (202) 477-6391
Web site: www.worldbank.org

The World Bank is a source of financial and technical assistance to developing countries around the world. The World Bank provides low-interest loans, interest-free credits, and grants to developing countries for a wide array of purposes that include investments in health, public administration, and infrastructure. Among the World Bank's publications is the report, *World Development Report 2009: Reshaping Economic Geography and World Development Indicators 2009.*

World Health Organization (WHO)
Avenue Appia 20, Geneva 27   1211
  Switzerland
41-22-791-2111 • fax: 41-22-791-3111

e-mail: info@who.int
Web site: www.who.int

WHO is the directing and coordinating authority for health within the United Nations system. WHO provides leadership on global health matters, providing technical support to countries and monitoring and assessing health trends. WHO compiles global health data and statistics, providing access to the WHO Statistical Information System (WHOSIS) at its Web site.

Bibliography

Books

Tony Barnett and Alan Whiteside — *AIDS in the Twenty-First Century: Disease and Globalization.* New York: Palgrave Macmillan, 2006.

Robert Calderisi — *The Trouble with Africa: Why Foreign Aid Isn't Working.* New York: Palgrave Macmillan, 2007.

Kondwani Chirambo — *The Political Cost of AIDS in Africa: Evidence from Six Countries.* Pretoria, South Africa: IDASA, 2008.

Deborah Dortzbach and W. Meredith Long — *The AIDS Crisis: What We Can Do.* Downers Grove, IL: InterVarsity Press, 2006.

Sammuel V. Duh — *Saving Africa From HIV/AIDS: We Can Do It.* Ghana: Afram, 2008.

Helen Epstein — *The Invisible Cure: Africa, the West, and the Fight Against AIDS.* New York: Farrar, Straus, and Giroux, 2007.

Nicole Itano — *No Place Left to Bury the Dead: Denial, Despair, and Hope in the African AIDS Pandemic.* New York: Atria, 2007.

Peris S. Jones — *AIDS Treatment and Human Rights in Context.* New York: Palgrave Macmillan, 2009.

Ezekiel Kalipeni, Karen Flynn, and Cynthia Pope, eds.

Strong Women, Dangerous Times: Gender and HIV/AIDS in Africa. Hauppauge, NY: Nova Science Publisher, 2009.

Stephen Lewis

Race Against Time: Searching for Hope in AIDS-Ravaged Africa. Toronto: House of Anansi Press, 2006.

Franklyn Lisk

Global Institutions and the HIV/AIDS Epidemic: Responding to an International Crisis. New York: Routledge, 2009.

Peter Mugyenyi

Genocide by Denial: How Profiteering from HIV/AIDS Killed Millions. Kampala, Uganda: Fountain Publishers, 2008.

Stephanie Nolen

28: Stories of AIDS in Africa. London: Portobello, 2007.

Nana K. Poku

AIDS in Africa: How the Poor Are Dying. Malden, MA: Polity Press, 2006.

Jonny Steinberg

Sizwe's Test: A Young Man's Journey Through Africa's AIDS Epidemic. New York: Simon & Schuster, 2008.

Periodicals

Doug Bandow

"The World Harm Organization," *American Spectator*, February 24, 2005.

Pamela Barnes and Nicholas Hellman — "This Pandemic Is Entirely Preventable," *Globe & Mail*, February 9, 2009.

Chris Beyrer and Voravit Suwanvanichkij — ". . . And in Another, AIDS in Retreat," *New York Times*, August 12, 2006.

Alan Brody — "In One Country, AIDS on the Rampage . . . ," *New York Times*, August 12, 2006.

David Brown — "Africa Gives 'ABC' Mixed Grades," *Washington Post*, August 15, 2006.

Chicago Tribune — "Focusing the Fight on AIDS," December 1, 2007.

Diane E. Dees — "Substantial Amount of AIDS Funding Goes to Religious Groups," *Mother Jones*, January 29, 2006.

Economist — "1.3 by 5: Treating AIDS," April 1, 2005.

Michael Fumento — "The African Heterosexual AIDS Myth," *Townhall.com*, April 14, 2005.

Richard Holbrooke — "Let's Scrap a Losing Strategy on AIDS," *The Star-Ledger (Newark, NJ)*, October 10, 2007.

Esther Kaplan — "Fairy-Tale Failure," *American Prospect*, July–August 2006.

Robert Knight — "AIDS: The Questions They Won't Ask," *Townhall.com*, November 30, 2007.

Nicholas D. Kristof   "When Marriage Kills," *New York Times*, March 30, 2005.

La Crosse Tribune   "The Faces of AIDS in the U.S. and Developing World," November 28, 2007.

Kathryn Jean Lopez   "Purpose-Driven AIDS Prevention," *National Review Online*, August 30, 2006.

Vivien Marx and Graham Lawton   "Circumcision: To Cut or Not to Cut?" *New Scientist*, July 16, 2008.

Andrew Meldrum   "AIDS Activist Turns South Africa Around," *Progressive*, May 2007.

Pramit Mitra   "AIDS: Facing the Second Wave," *YaleGlobal Online*, January 20, 2005.

Daniel P. Moloney   "From Good Intentions to Bad AIDS Policy: The Moral Hazards of Redesigning PEPFAR," Heritage Foundation WebMemo #1921, May 13, 2008.

New York Times   "The Global AIDS Fight," February 29, 2008.

Jeremiah Norris   "Blame It on Rio," *National Review Online*, March 30, 2005.

Babatunde Osotimehin   "The Other Half," *New York Times*, August 19, 2005.

Thomas C. Quinn   "HIV/AIDS in Women: An Expanding Epidemic," *Science*, June 10, 2005.

Andrew Rice   "An African Solution," *Nation*, June
                   11, 2007.

Deborah Roberts   "My Firsthand View of AIDS in
                   Africa," *Ebony*, January 2007.

Michael J. Selgelid "Infectious Diseases, Security, and
and Christian   Ethics: The Case of HIV/AIDS,"
Enemark   *Bioethics*, November 2008.

Beatrice Were   "The Destructive Strings of U.S. Aid:
                   The Stigma of AIDS," *International
                   Herald Tribune*, December 16, 2005.

World Health   "Towards Universal Access: Scaling
Organization,   Up Priority HIV/AIDS Interventions
UNAIDS, and   in the Health Sector," World Health
UNICEF   Organization, 2008.

Index